M000079011

An Introduction to Spirituality

SPIRITUALITY FOR LIFE

Kim Bentley

Copyright © Kim Bentley 2021

Published in Australia by Altruistec Publishing

Altruistec
Publishing

All rights reserved. No part of this publication may be reproduced or transmitted in any form or by any means, electronic or mechanical, including photocopying, recording, or any information storage or retrieval system, without prior permission from the author.

Publisher's Cataloging-in-Publication Data

Names: Bentley, Kim.
Title: An introduction to spirituality : spirituality for life / Kim Bentley.
Description: Melbourne, Australia : Altruistec Publishing, 2022. | Contains 14 color diagrams. | Summary: Focuses on facilitating spiritual growth by covering concepts such as core spiritual principles, the Divine and our relationship with the Divine, creation, love and wisdom, goodness and truth, our emotions, temptations, consciousness, the spirit world, and death.
Identifiers: ISBN 9780645281507 (pbk.) | ISBN 9780645281514 (ebook)
Subjects: LCSH: Conduct of life. | Self-actualization (Psychology). | Spiritual formation. | Spiritual life. | BISAC: BODY, MIND & SPIRIT / General. | BODY, MIND & SPIRIT / Inspiration & Personal Growth. | RELIGION / Spirituality.
Classification: LCC BL624 B46 2022 (print) | LCC BL624 (ebook) | DDC 291.44 B--dc23

Acknowledgements

This book could not have been completed to its final form without the help and input from many good people.

I am very grateful and thankful to the following readers for reviewing the preliminary versions of the text and providing valuable feedback during its writing: Rev. David Moffat, Rev. David Millar, Michael Burke, Tammy Kuch, Donna Kuch, Sammi Gregory-Tacey, Helena Steel, and Shannine Curran. Thanks also to Karl Forssling for his excellent work on the cover layouts for the book. It has also been great to have Julie Burbidge provide guidance with some copyright and referencing matters, and I'm very grateful to Michelle Bansen for her assistance finding a suitable publisher.

I would also like to acknowledge the late Rev. Christopher Skinner for his friendship, guidance, and introduction to Swedenborg's works. Prior to the writing of this book we co-authored the booklet *Introduction to Spirituality* with some of this material having been integrated into this text. And last but not least, I'd like to thank my lovely wife Jackie Caldwell for her patience and support throughout the writing of this book.

Kim Bentley

Forward

I am a professional engineer and qualified careers practitioner who became sensitive to spirituality in my early forties. For over a decade since then I have learnt and applied universal spiritual principles and concepts in my life. In doing so I have become more centred, peaceful, joyful, caring and considerate, loving, reassured, and less anxious about the future - experiencing great spiritual growth. This has motivated me to write this introductory book to share core spiritual principles and concepts, and how our humanity changes as we develop spiritually, so you too might also benefit on your journey.

We are so much more than the physical body we see with our physical sight. As you read this book you will learn about your full humanity that comprises your soul, higher mind, lower mind, auric field (containing several invisible bodies, chakras and meridians), and physical body. You will learn how each of these areas of our being forms an energetic system that makes us so very special and allows us to tap into the infinite stream of Consciousness from the Divine. This influx of energy from the Divine flows down through our being's various levels. Ultimately, we experience our everyday states of consciousness giving us our unique perspective of the physical world.

You will gain an understanding of universal spiritual principles and concepts along with the very important process of spiritual development. You will also come to appreciate some of the changes in your aura's invisible bodies and chakras that take place as you grow spiritually and that this benefits your mental and physical health. You will learn about consciousness and how it relates to your current state and possible future states of spiritual growth. This knowledge will equip you to see your life with greater perspective and clarity of the fundamental reality that you are at all times a spiritual being living a spiritual life clothed in a physical body in the physical world. Finally, you will gain some knowledge of what takes place spiritually when we die and what life is like in the spiritual world.

This book is not intended to be a step-by-step guide for everyday spiritual practices. It is intended to give you a good understanding of what makes you human and the spiritual principles and concepts that govern our lives so you can live and appreciate spirituality in a holistic manner. This knowledge will form the foundation to enable you to become more loving, wise, joyful, peaceful, and fulfilled in your physical life into the future, and for your life thereafter. May this book help to inspire you and enlighten you in more ways than mere knowledge.

Kim Bentley

Emanuel Swedenborg – A Brief Overview

Emanuel Swedenborg was born in 1688, the son of a Lutheran Bishop in Sweden, and was a great scientist, engineer, inventor, author, seer and mystic. He was evaluated by Stanford University (by applying the Stanford-Binet Intelligence Scales test) to be one of history's three greatest intellects along with John Stuart Mill and Johann Wolfgang von Goethe. Philosopher Ralph Waldo Emerson, author Helen Keller, and poet Jorge Luis Borges all concluded that Swedenborg possessed an unparalleled genius.

Swedenborg's scientific and engineering achievements include: the proposal of an atomic theory of matter; was first to propose a nebular theory as the origin for our solar system; was first to correctly identify the function of the cerebral cortex and the ductless glands; was first to deduce correctly that brain waves moved synchronously with the lungs and not with the heart; was a pioneer in magnetism theory; wrote extensive works on metallurgy; designed and oversaw construction of what is still the world's largest dry-dock; and invented the first rational design for an aeroplane.

He devoted twenty-five years of full-time service to Sweden's industrial development working in its mining industry. He spent several years travelling around Europe and meeting with the greatest minds in all known fields of science at the time, later becoming Sweden's Chief Astronomer. He also learned nine languages, served in Sweden's House of Nobles for fifty years, and was deeply respected by both sides of parliament for his work on monetary and fiscal policy.

While his scientific and engineering career progressed, he developed an ever-growing and consuming need to find the seat of the human soul. In 1744 at 56 years of age, he reached a defining moment in his life when he experienced a number of dreams and visions that profoundly moved him, recording them in a dream journal. From these dreams, he learnt to overcome his pride in his achievements by acknowledging all merit to his Creator. This was not only the key but seems to have been the final doorway leading into a paranormal residence in spiritual realms. On Easter Day in 1744, Swedenborg experienced a Christ vision of such extraordinary power that it changed his outer life dramatically. As an outcome of this, he put aside all activities in natural science in favour of writing and publishing a new spiritual understanding of life.

From then on, his inner life underwent an extraordinary paranormal transition leaving him with a capacity for awareness of the spiritual world that is totally unique in the annals of psychic phenomena. This ability was present daily for the remaining twenty-seven years of his life and allowed him to produce his crowning works. By the time of his death, he had used his careful observational style learned as a scientist, to write thirty volumes of completely unique spiritual books that captured his experiences and explained his findings, so others may be enlightened to live in heavenly ways. He also enunciated universal spiritual principles that can equally be applied in Christian and non-Christian contexts and showed the link between the physical and spiritual worlds, and how life here is a preparation for the eternal life to come.

Contents

1 Humanity and Spiritual Growth

Have you ever wondered what it means to be to be a human being? Have you ever considered the possibility that we are so much more than the physical body that we live with? This is a powerful thought which can often lead us to knowledge and understanding about who we are. All spiritual teachings tell us that we are not our physical body, but rather we have a physical body that we use.

1.1 We as human beings

We as a human being are a spirit with a spiritual body that manifests a physical body to enable us to live in the physical world. Our total makeup as a human being comprises our soul, spirit with spiritual body, invisible physical body, and our physical body - we will explore this further in chapter 2. Our spiritual body allows us to live in the spiritual world. Usually we are not conscious of our spiritual body. However, we can experience the spiritual world consciously on some level in our life by developing ourselves as we learn and apply spiritual principles throughout our life. Doing so allows us at times to recognise the source of our thoughts and feelings, being either from a higher place or from a selfish place.

Our spirit is constantly developing as we live our life in this world. It is God's desire that we take His influence into our spirit and grow throughout our physical life. This opportunity for spiritual growth is the prime purpose of our physical life. Our spirit lives on to eternity, unlike our physical body. When our physical body dies, we (the spirit) become fully conscious of the spiritual dimension. We then continue to live there in a community with other spirits.

1.2 Our gifts and talents

We have all been created by God as individuals with a unique composition of gifts, talents, and other qualities that are meant to fit into the grand tapestry of humanity and be used throughout life's journey for the greatest good of all.

A talent can be defined as a naturally occurring set of aptitudes gifted to us, and enables us to learn, develop, and perform in some particular manner to a higher level than other people who do not possess our talent.

Aptitudes

Aptitudes can be physical, emotional, or mental. Aptitude is our inborn potential to learn to do certain kinds of tasks or work at a certain level.

Ability is developed knowledge, understanding, learned or acquired skills or attitudes. When we have an aptitude for something then we will develop an ability to do it much faster, easier, and to a higher level than when we lack such an aptitude.

Our talents give us an in-built 'accelerated pathway' to enable greater understanding and skill development compared to learning for a person who does not possess such talents. We all need to find that 'accelerated pathway' and then guide our learning and development along that pathway. Our talent will enable the learning of a superior way of doing something or mental and emotional processing, and our strengths will be developed according to our level of sustained interest and activity deploying that talent.

God gives us a unique set of talents that He wants us to draw upon to build strengths by performing good uses for the greatest benefit of all. As we do this we will grow in wisdom and heavenly love while being of utmost service to our 'community' doing what we love. After all, each of us has a unique role or life purpose that God wants us to perform both here and in heaven.

1.3 Our strengths and use

Studies have shown that in general, people who 'volunteer' in the community tend to be happier, more fulfilled, and feel that their life is more meaningful. It is through our actions to be of use to others and ourselves in a selfless manner that we make use of our talents, through our strengths, to realise the greatest good for all. We add the greatest quality to our life and to the lives of others when we act with good intent. When we see others from a selfless perspective, we find the world to be a better place. We appreciate other people's gifts and see their benefit to others and themselves.

However, coming from a selfish perspective prevents us from seeing how we can offer and apply our gifts to others for mutual good. When we apply our talents and strengths with a selfish motive, we experience selfish pleasure. However, we turn away from God and separate our self from others and then suffer from negative emotions such as guilt, shame, and fear that result from these selfish activities.

1.4 Our life purpose

We are born into this world with untapped potential to develop our spirit or loving nature – which must be done in total freedom. Along our journey, God wants us to make use of our gifted talents to develop our strengths and use them for the greatest good of all. In doing so we live a life of good use doing the things we love and are uniquely suited to, while being of utmost benefit to our 'community.' The result being that we come to know and love the heavenly life here in this world, and then in the spiritual world, in heaven after we die.

Good and Evil:

Good or goodness takes place when we act from a motivation of love or wellbeing for everyone and everything, including ourself. We consider and do what we believe is best for all, even though our actions may not please all concerned. When we act from goodness we create positive outcomes in our life and in the lives of others and creation in general.

Evil takes place when we act from a motivation of selfish love. This means acting based on our own self-interest with no consideration of what is good for others or the rest of creation. In this case we turn away and separate from God, others, creation, and become destructive in our actions.

We grow spiritually when we embrace Divine Will and act in ways that are harmonious with Divine Providence. Our lives will be blessed when we do live in accord with the Divine plan as we understand it to be, if not in the short-term, then ultimately. Even if we do act contrary to the Divine plan, God works tirelessly giving us countless opportunities to return to the stream of Providence. In this world we always remain open to the possibility of misfortune, but that will not be detrimental to our eternal welfare if we respond

4

positively to these apparently adverse circumstances. We are born with inclinations towards selfishness, which if left to develop unchecked will eventually dominate our whole being, leading us towards evil. For us to develop our spirit or loving nature, we need to achieve a transformation of our inner being. We do this by consistently resisting opportunities for selfishness, and in doing so enhancing and transforming our spirit in the process over a lifetime of choices and change.

Throughout our life we choose to accept or reject the kind of life God offers us by making choices between good and evil, right and wrong. However, we can make our choices for many different reasons. In some situations, our motives can be altruistic, while at other times our motives can be quite selfish even though it appears we are doing 'good'. Most importantly, Swedenborg (see page iii) explains that God regards our aim or intention as being of utmost importance. Whatever our thoughts and deeds may be, varying in countless ways, they are all good provided our intent is good. But if our intent is bad, they are all bad.

> *Our aim or intention from moment-to-moment ultimately determines our very life.*

1.5 Motivation to grow spiritually

There are many reasons for people to be motivated to lead a spiritual life. We may feel at times that our life lacks purpose and meaning which can lead us to turn to God to develop a deeper relationship with Him, find answers, and experience a more satisfying life. At other times we may see the exquisite beauty and wonder in nature leading us to a belief in God. Some people may have had experiences with spirits, leading them to want to explore and develop spiritually.

5

Others have been brought up with religious teachings that have made a lasting impact on them in their lives.

Sometimes in our life we hit 'rock bottom' or we suffer from the ill effects of evil actions by ourselves or others, motivating us to embrace a life of spiritual development. Some people have become active in their spiritual journey after experiencing the death of a loved one. Others have met spiritually developed people who have inspired them to lead a spiritual life. We might choose to develop our self so we can serve God better and enjoy His love and wisdom.

Once we embark on our active spiritual journey, we will want to make good choices and develop a truer and stronger conscience. In doing so we will experience both inner and outer contentment, peace, happiness, and joy. When we actively persevere to consistently grow spiritually, we are on the road to a heavenly life after we die, when our conscious awareness shifts to the spiritual world. We do not have to wait until after we die to experience heavenly joy and happiness. We can achieve these things and contentment throughout this life by consistently learning spiritual truths and applying them through goodness in our life.

1.6 Benefits of spiritual growth

As we grow spiritually to become more loving and wise people, we can benefit in many ways:

Some Benefits of Spiritual Growth:			
Joy, happiness, peace, and contentment	Improved mental and physical health	Stronger and deeper friendships	Loving relationships with others

We can experience some form of pleasure during the release of spiritual energy or influx when we are motivated in thought, words, or movement. The source of this pleasure can be hellish (evil or selfish motivation) or heavenly (for the greater good of all). If the source is heavenly, we can experience happiness, or joy, or serenity, or some other positive emotion and feeling from the conjunction or simultaneous joining of goodness and truth.

However, when the source of our pleasure is hellish, we can seem to experience happiness, however, our pleasure will eventually transform into negative emotions and feelings such as guilt or shame as a result of the selfish act. Evil spirits stir up our hellish (selfish) loves (comprised of many evils) that are linked through our memories of past selfish (evil) actions to generate negative emotions, feelings, and self-talk that we experience consciously.

> **Joy:**
> Joy is the affection that comes from within and is expressed as intense happiness, delight, and bliss.

True happiness and joy arise when we perform uses for others and ourselves with an intent directed towards the greater good of all. When this takes place, we see good things that are happening to others and ourselves separate from our own selfish needs. We also become happier when we sense happiness and joy in others. We experience greater pleasure in doing good for others for its own sake. Happiness occurs when we bring joy into the lives of others rather than selfishly accumulating ever more material possessions or satisfying our ego in other ways.

True happiness and joy are also felt when we see others succeed with their good goals and we share or contribute to experiences where the utmost welfare and wellbeing of all is the prime focus.

1.7 What is spiritual growth?

Our spirit is connected to God who powers our life and provides us with a spiritual environment whereby we have freewill under His Providence. This allows us to accept or reject His energy or influx - being love of all and wisdom. When we reject His influx, we instead take into our being hellish influx from the hells – being selfish love and foolishness. Here love refers to the spiritual energy and substance that motivates and provides for creation (heavenly love) or destruction (hellish love). Divine love or heavenly love is love of all for the greater good of all. Hellish love is love of one's self for one's selfish ends with complete disregard to God, all people, and all of creation. Spiritual growth takes place when we choose heavenly influx into our being instead of hellish influx.

Growing spiritually involves resisting temptations to be selfish and instead choosing loving affections, thoughts, and actions. For us to be able to resist temptations, we firstly need to learn spiritual truths and in doing so rationally understand them. When we rationally understand them, we not only remember them, but we actually understand how they apply to our life. Then we can from this rational understanding see our false beliefs and selfishness for what they really are. From this position we can then resist our selfish desires by living what we understand to be true through goodness in our physical life. This opens the door for God to implant and unite genuine truth along with genuine goodness into our spirit.

Through consistently resisting temptations, God gives us more of His love and wisdom, goodness and truth into our spirit. As this happens our love and wisdom grows and is enhanced, and we allow God or Spirit to work through us more powerfully as we live our life. We then develop a truer and stronger conscience and a higher level of consciousness. This then importantly gives us a greater ability to see the overall reality of the world around us.

Everything good and true in our being is from God.

As we grow spiritually, we experience more peace, joy, happiness, and faith. Swedenborg states that the final state of our spiritual development at the time of our death determines our spiritual home to eternity. As such, it is vitally important to develop spiritually as fully as possible during our physical life!

Spiritual growth is explained in greater detail in section 5.3.

2 Invisible and Physical Self

Each of us are unique across time to eternity. No one who ever lives will be exactly like us, however, we will all share varying degrees of wonderful aspects gifted to us from the Divine. As previously stated, we are much more than our physical selves. We are an amazing and complex energy system energised in various ways from the spiritual world and from the physical world. Our spiritual, mental, emotional, and physical wellbeing is directly affected by our innate ability to receive and distribute this energy throughout our being. In this chapter we will come to appreciate how wonderful our humanity really is.

2.1 Our human makeup

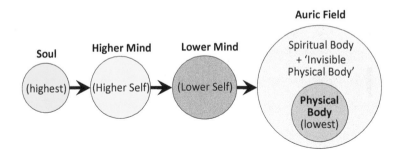

Figure 1 Basic model of our humanity.

Although we have a body, we are much more than our body as can be seen in Figure 1. It is our *mind* and not our brain that makes us our person. We are comprised of our soul, our higher mind or higher self which Swedenborg calls our spiritual mind, lower mind or lower self which Swedenborg calls our natural mind, our auric field containing our spiritual body and 'invisible physical body', and our physical body.

Note that our auric field is a template from which our physical body manifests.

Our mind is comprised of our higher mind and our lower mind. Our higher mind receives spiritual energy or influx from the Divine via our soul. Our lower mind receives influx from our higher mind and also from angels with us or evil spirits with us according to our intention. Our conscious awareness derives from our lower mind. Note that our lower mind is not our brain. After influx flows through our lower mind, it flows into our auric field where it is changed in form. Then it flows into our body and brain; cerebellum (used as part of the generation of our emotions) and finally into our cerebrum (used as part of the generation of our thoughts and ideas). Swedenborg describes our brain as the organ that allows our mind to ultimately act through our body as a whole. It functions along with our auric field to interface our mind with our body.

Our Soul

Our soul is the very core and most inner and deepest part of our being. God connects with us through our soul and through this connection provides our spirit with life force to eternity, hence our immortality. Our soul is made of purer spiritual essence than our mind and exists on a higher spiritual level or plane than our mind. It is above our mind and therefore it is above our conscious awareness. We cannot corrupt our soul since spiritual energy or influx always flows from higher levels or planes to lower levels or planes, being transformed on each transition. Spiritual energy or influx flows from God into our soul, then into our higher mind, and then into our lower mind, and finally into our auric field and then into our physical body. Our soul ultimately governs our body's form and spontaneous

12

processes of growth and nutrition. It also stores the scenarios of our life including those of our emotions, feelings, thoughts, and actions, and is the medium by which our conscience and spiritual levels of our mind are developed by God as we live.

There are two inherent capabilities in our soul that allow us to be a human being: **freewill** and **rationality**. Freewill refers to our ongoing ability to freely choose between spiritually healthy or unhealthy options. Rationality refers to our ability to see life relative to our eternal spiritual welfare. In other words, the ability to evaluate the spiritual influences that are ongoing in our life - as a result we are able to evaluate and make spiritual choices as we live. It is in our mind that we use our soul's capabilities of freewill and rationality and in the process we experience various states of conscious awareness as a result of our states of consciousness (explained in chapter 6).

Our spirit

Many of us are unaware that our spirit exists on several levels and comprises our higher mind, lower mind, and spiritual body:

- Our *higher mind* or higher self is the real, true core of our being where love, feelings, ideas, and wisdom of heavenly nature originate, powered by Divine energy. It is the invisible and superconscious (above conscious awareness) part of our spirit and is the foundation of all the good that has been created in our lives.

- Our *lower mind* or lower self is that part of our spirit that allows us to express our desires and realise our intentions and have conscious awareness of our world. Our lower mind is influenced by both heavenly and

13

hellish love, feelings, and thoughts from angels and evil spirits with us.

- Our **spiritual body** is not part of our mind. It makes up the 'higher' components of our auric field. Our spiritual body has a head, eyes, ears, torso, arms, hands, and feet, etc., like our physical body, except it is made of spiritual substance. Its form corresponds to the makeup of our mind (human and beautiful if our mind is predominantly angelic, and monstrous if our mind is predominantly evil). It acts as a medium for the generation of the higher aspects of our mental, emotional, and will functionality. It is only visible to our spiritual senses. Swedenborg writes in his book Heaven and Hell that angels can see the events in our life by examining our spiritual body.

2.2 Flow of influx into us

Swedenborg explains that God is Love itself, Wisdom itself, and Life itself, being Consciousness. Life from God flows from the highest spiritual level or plane down to the lowest level being the natural level. Therefore, God's Life flows down from the highest heaven, the celestial (third) heaven, nearest God, to and through the spiritual (second) heaven, and then the spiritual-natural (first) heaven, and into the lowest level, nature. God's Life also flows through the heavens and into the hells. God's Wisdom governs and provides for all things.

God disposes, regulates, tempers, and moderates all things in the heavens and hells, and through the heavens and hells all things in the physical world. We are connected to and receive influx from both the heavens and the hells in order for us to have freewill, grow spiritually, and live. Life or influx from God flows into us in successive order as shown in Figure 2 ahead.

> **Influx (Spiritual Energy Flow):**
>
> Swedenborg, *Heaven and Hell*
>
> Influx is spiritual energy flow. Divine influx is God's Love (or Goodness on a finer scale) and Wisdom (or Truth on a finer scale) flowing to all of creation which comes into our soul directly from God and then flows into our higher mind.
>
> Hellish influx is hellish love (being selfish – or evil on a finer scale) and foolishness (or falsity on a finer scale) flowing in from evil spirits. We perceive hellish influx as selfish desires, negative emotions, feelings, thoughts, and actions that try to disrupt and destroy us and others spiritually and physically.
>
> Our mind is also influenced by Divine influx coming indirectly to us from angels with us and by hellish influx from evil spirits with us. This influx happens at all times and is essential for our mind and our physical body to function.
>
> The Divine influx flowing in from angels works with influx from our higher mind to generate our conscience. When we choose to take Divine influx into our mind, it gives us love, wisdom, goodness, and truth. We perceive this influx as altruistic affections, positive emotions, feelings, thoughts, and actions.

Our soul (the innermost part of our being and the highest spiritual substance) receives influx directly from God. Influx flowing into our soul is transformed and then flows into our higher mind. It is then transformed by our higher mind and passes into our lower mind. In all moments our lower mind is subjected to two more sources of influx from the spiritual world: i) from angels we are connected and associated with; and ii) from evil spirits we are connected and associated with.

Our lower mind transforms the influx from our higher mind according to our intention (enabled through freewill):

- If our intention is goodness, then influx from our higher mind flowing into our lower mind is united in a positive way with the influx from angels with us. This resulting influx will be goodness and truth that enhances our mind, auric field, and physical body.

- If our intention is evil (being selfish), then less influx from our higher mind will flow into our lower mind and will be distorted by influx from evil spirits with us. Some goodness and truth our lower mind receives from our higher mind is transformed into evil and falsity. This is detrimental to our mind, auric field, and physical body.

The resulting influx transformed by our lower mind, along with universal influx from other beings, then passes into our auric field's invisible bodies via all our chakras and meridians (explained in sections 2.4 and 2.5). Our auric field transforms this influx and manifests our physical body. Some of this influx then passes into our physical body (brain and other parts of our body) and we experience emotions, feelings, thoughts, and actions. Our physical body is lowest in order and also receives influx from God through the physical world.

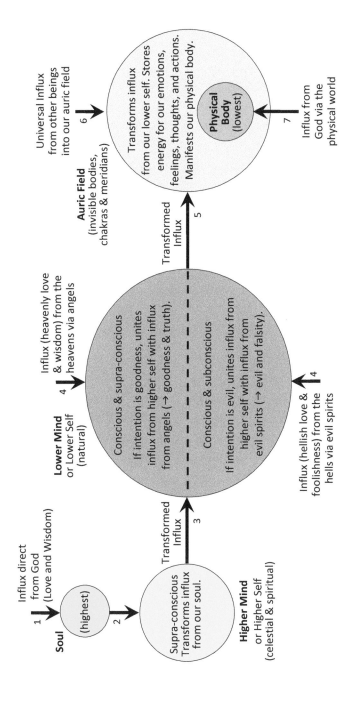

Figure 2 Influx into our soul, mind, auric field, and physical body.

Influx direct from God (Love and Wisdom)

1

Soul

(highest)

2

Transformed Influx

3

Higher Mind or Higher Self (celestial & spiritual)

Supra-conscious Transforms influx from our soul.

Influx (heavenly love & wisdom) from the heavens via angels

4

Lower Mind or Lower Self (natural)

Conscious & supra-conscious

If intention is goodness, unites influx from higher self with influx from angels (→ goodness & truth).

Conscious & subconscious

If intention is evil, unites influx from higher self with influx from evil spirits (→ evil and falsity).

Influx (hellish love & foolishness) from the hells via evil spirits

4

Transformed Influx

5

Universal Influx from other beings into our auric field

6

Auric Field (invisible bodies, chakras & meridians)

Transforms influx from our lower self. Stores energy for our emotions, feelings, thoughts, and actions. Manifests our physical body.

Physical Body (lowest)

Influx from God via the physical world

7

17

2.3 Our mind

Swedenborg explains that our mind is an organ of consciousness. This means that our mind gives us access to perceive a finite portion of the Divine's infinite Reality at any one time – a truly amazing realisation! Our mind like our soul is made of spiritual substance, unlike our brain which is made of physical substance. Note that spiritual substance cannot be detected by physical equipment or our physical senses. We can only ever detect spiritual substance using our spiritual senses that have been opened. This is because spiritual substance exists on a higher and more subtle dimension or plane than physical substance. For us to make use of our spiritual senses we must develop our mind through spiritual practices.

Swedenborg states that our mind receives love and wisdom directly from God and indirectly through the medium of the world of spirits - by thoughts and feelings flowing in from its inhabitants. The world of spirits or intermediate realm lies 'below' heaven and 'above' hell and is the medium between the two. This is where we have association with angels and evil spirits so that God can give us freewill to make spiritual choices. It is where our spirit bodies exist while we live as human beings. It looks so much like the physical world, that some spirits when they initially pass over after death think they are still in the physical world. It is there that we have balanced influence from angels and evil spirits and hence are given freewill to develop our loving nature. Swedenborg repeatedly states that throughout our entire life our mind is in the spiritual world being subjected to good and evil spiritual influences.

2.3.1 The three levels of our mind

As explained earlier, our mind is comprised of our higher mind and our lower mind – both made of spiritual substance and part of our spirit (which includes our spiritual body). Our mind has three discrete levels of mental activity as shown in Figure 3.

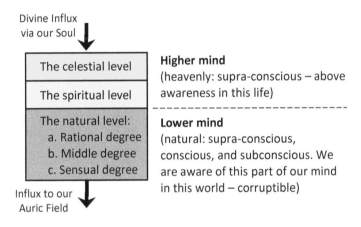

Figure 3 The three distinct levels of our mind.

Rev. Douglas Taylor in his book *The Hidden Levels of The Mind* explains that Swedenborg describes our *higher mind* as being comprised of two distinct **levels** of mental activity (celestial and spiritual). These two levels receive influx from the Divine via our soul. Our *lower mind* has a natural level being our third level of mental activity in our mind; it receives influx from both angels and evil spirits. These three levels exist independently and are not intertwined, yet they operate together to form our functioning mind.

Our higher mind is supra-conscious (above our conscious awareness) with our celestial and spiritual levels corresponding to the celestial and spiritual angelic heavens respectively. Our higher mind contains only spiritual substances being goodness and truths that are God's.

Love and Wisdom, Goodness and Truth:

Divine Love is motivating spiritual energy and substance that is comprised of many ordered and related goodness.

Wisdom is also spiritual substance that directs the form of creation and is comprised of many ordered and related truths.

Wisdom embodies the means to direct love to create good use while on a finer scale, truth embodies the means to direct goodness to create good use.

Our influence from God comes through our higher mind. It receives love and wisdom and goodness and truth which belongs to God. From this influx we perceive life in a heavenly way. When we act with good intention, we exercise our higher mind and draw upon angelic influence. Our higher mind brings affections or goodness and truths into our lower mind which we experience as positive emotions, feelings, thoughts, ideas, and actions. In doing so, we allow our higher mind or true self to be expressed in our daily life.

Our *celestial* level is the highest level of our higher mind and receives the purest and highest level of love and truth from God. We are drawing upon and enhancing the celestial level of our mind when we are following God's commandments; in particular the first commandment "You shall love God with all your heart, with all your soul, and with all your mind" (Matt. 22:37). "He who has my commandments and keeps them, it is he who loves me" (John 14:21). Following

God's commandments is to live a life according to Divine Truth and therefore being in alignment with the Divine. In this case we are loving God most dearly.

Our *spiritual* level of our higher mind is 'below' the celestial level. It receives love and truth from God that allows us to have love for others and feelings of goodwill or charity. We exercise the second of the two greatest commandments when we draw upon this love and truth in our mind; "You shall love your neighbour as yourself" (Matt. 22:39). Here love refers to loving the goodness and truth that is God's in others regardless whether we like them or not.

During our physical life we have very little awareness of our higher mind. However, if after passing into the spiritual world we become an angel, we will possess the wisdom belonging to that kingdom of heaven (celestial or spiritual) corresponding to whichever part of our higher mind we were most disposed to use before we passed on.

Our *natural* level of our lower mind is of lower spiritual substance than the celestial or spiritual levels of our higher mind and receives supra-conscious, conscious, and subconscious influx. It is the lowest level of our mind. Note that our brain is not our lower mind. Our brain is our physical organ that our mind uses. It allows us to function in the physical world. We are a spirit and our lower mind refers to that part of us that provides us with our conscious affections (goodness) and selfish desires (evils), and cognitions (truths) and delusions (falsities).

Our lower mind receives supra-conscious and conscious heavenly influx being affections and truths (some of which we experience as positive emotions, feelings, and thoughts) in two ways: i) directly from God via our higher mind; and ii) indirectly from angels with us. Conversely, our lower mind receives subconscious and conscious influx from evil spirits with us, being hellish (selfish) desires and falsities (some of which we experience as negative emotions, feelings, and thoughts.

2.3.2 Lower mind

Swedenborg explains that the natural level of our lower mind is comprised of three degrees: sensual (lowest), middle, and rational (highest). Note that the separate *levels* of our mind (celestial, spiritual, and natural) operate uniquely due to the different quality of the love that motivates them. However, the *degrees* of our natural level are defined by the different functions that each one performs.

Our three functional degrees develop in conjunction with each other as we grow from infants and represent the main three stages of mental growth of our lower mind. Typically, their functions relate to our everyday physical, worldly life that is often dominated by self-centredness. We develop these functional degrees as we enhance our physical coordination, and gain physical, scientific, and spiritual knowledge and understanding.

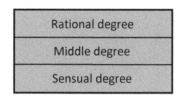

Figure 4 The degrees within our lower mind's natural level.

Rev. D. Taylor in his book *The Hidden Levels of The Mind* explains the functions of our three degrees of our lower mind. In summary they are:

- *Sensation:* develops the *sensual degree* of our lower mind (the lowest degree of our lower mind). Starting from babies, we make use of our five senses to develop this part of our lower mind.

- *Generalisation:* develops our *middle degree* of our lower mind. We form relationships or conclusions about the events relating to people and things in our physical world based on the information entering our mind using our senses.

- *Sense of proportion or rational:* develops our *rational degree* of our lower mind (the highest degree of our lower mind). This function gives us the ability to distinguish or see the ratio between natural and spiritual concepts.

Our lower mind is only a small part of our overall mind. While our higher mind is mostly above our conscious awareness, our lower mind gives us our everyday conscious awareness which is why we associate our self so much with this part of us.

Sensual degree

As previously stated, our sensory learnings begin as growing babies. Swedenborg teaches that as babies develop, celestial angels from the highest heaven are present with them, and gently unconsciously influence and give them heavenly delights of goodness and truth of a celestial nature, whenever they are not self-conscious. This takes place as their minds are receiving stimulation from their senses during caressing, comforting, or when falling asleep.

Swedenborg refers to this reception of influx from angels into their minds as "remains of goodness and truth." These gifts in babies' minds become the basis for the future development of children's heavenly qualities, being love and affection, wisdom and truth. God ensures that we are all gifted with these remains so that we can have the opportunity to develop spiritually as we progress through life, no matter what our upbringing.

Later as infants mature into children, their sensory levels develop further as they continue to be stimulated with sensory images of things that they experience through their senses of sight, hearing, touch, taste, and smell. As this takes place their understanding is also formed. The sensory images remain in the child's natural memory and are recalled in their future life to form their imagination.

Middle degree

As a child develops, they are exploring the world around them, and discovering what people do and think, and how things in the world behave. This is a development beyond just learning through their senses. They are making generalisations about people and things from their interactions with the world. They are forming rules and relationships from what their senses tell them. In doing so, they are making more and more use of their middle degree of their lower mind. As they mature, the development of their middle degree forms the foundation for the future development of the rational degree of their lower mind.

The rational degree

The sensory and middle degrees of our lower mind can be developed from experiencing the world through interaction using our senses and forming rules or relationships from these experiences. To develop the highest part of our lower mind (our rational degree) requires going beyond learning from our senses. We need to develop an understanding of the relationships between the physical world and the spiritual world. We do this by gaining knowledge of spiritual principles and teachings, ideally done by learning from sacred texts such as the Bible.

For most people, their rational degree begins to develop as they progress from children to young adults when they are starting to live moral or spiritual principles in their life. At a later stage in life, if we embark on a journey of spiritual development, we will open our rational degree to the action of our higher mind and have our higher mind operate to develop our lower mind. We do this by cooperating with God to apply the spiritual principles we have learnt in our daily life through altruistic practices of service.

Our will and understanding, desire and delusion

Each of the three degrees of our lower mind (rational, middle, and sensual) has an inner heavenly part and an outer natural part as shown in Figure 5 ahead. Our inner heavenly part has a faculty known as the will that works with our motivations or wants and a thinking faculty known as the understanding. Our outer natural part has desire (selfish) in place of the will and delusion in place of understanding.

In our lower mind, our will is the home of our heavenly loves and affections or goodness, and our understanding is the home of our wisdom and truths. Our will and understanding work together and operate on all three degrees of our lower mind (rational, middle, and sensual). Our will is largely outside our conscious awareness. It receives and works with our heavenly loves (that we experience as positive emotions) or on a finer scale, our affections or goodness (that we experience as positive feelings) that we have made our own and impulses that drive us.

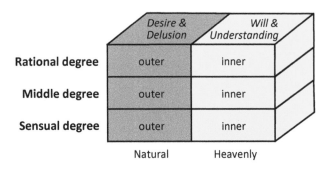

	Desire & Delusion	Will & Understanding	
Rational degree	outer	inner	
Middle degree	outer	inner	
Sensual degree	outer	inner	
	Natural	Heavenly	

Figure 5 Our lower mind's inner heavenly and outer natural parts.

If we are being selfish then we are not using our will (which receives heavenly love and on a finer scale, goodness) but instead using our desire (selfish), which is the home of our hellish loves (and on a finer scale, evils) that we experience as negative emotions and feelings. Our desire works with our delusion (the opposite of our understanding) which is the home of our falsity. Anything we think, say, or otherwise do at any given moment is driven by our will or our desire. Although, our will or our desire does not command our automatic instinctual responses.

Our understanding or intellect is the part of our mind that receives wisdom, and on a finer scale truth, that we have made our own. Our understanding perceives reality and from that we experience sensation. It processes information, generates thoughts and ideas, and imagines outcomes for good use. Our true intelligence and knowledge derives from our understanding. And most importantly, our understanding is the mechanism that allows our will to be made more angelic. Whereas our will can be largely outside our conscious awareness, our understanding is that part of our conscious mind that gives us our conscious awareness of reality. Our understanding knows without reasoning: truths, causes of things, their connections, and order of relationship of the things we experience and have knowledge of. It is the source of our perception or intuition.

When we are motivated by our will (through goodness), our understanding directs our good deeds (thoughts, words, and actions). Our understanding is what we use to resist our selfish desires and hence grow spiritually. Our will and understanding are developed whenever we learn and apply spiritual truths in our life in a loving manner while resisting our selfish urges, thoughts, and actions.

The quality of our being is a result of the love in our will and the wisdom in our understanding.

When we choose angelic influence from the angels around us, love and wisdom (and on a finer scale, goodness and truth) from angels with us, and from God via our higher mind, is received into our will and understanding in our lower mind. In this case we are exercising spiritual power in our life and growing spiritually. However, when we are motivated by hellish love (or on a finer scale evil) and thinking false thoughts, we are not making use of our will or understanding since our will works with goodness and our understanding works with truth. In this instance we are using our desire with a distorted comprehension of information. Our mind is being motivated by evil and we are thinking irrationally from some degree of delusion. We are not being wise, intelligent, or rational but instead being foolish, manipulative or cunning, irrational, and being destructive in our life. Note that this restricts and distorts influx from our higher mind, corrupts our lower mind, and is detrimental to our auric field and physical health.

2.4 Our invisible bodies and physical body

As explained earlier, the energy from the Divine and the spiritual world passes through our mind and then into our auric field and finally into our physical body. Our amazing auric field comprises seven invisible bodies of ever-increasing vibrational frequency (as shown in Figure 6 ahead). It transforms and stores energy from our mind and passes it to our body to facilitate our physical functioning and abilities.

Our innermost three auric bodies (etheric body, emotional body, and mental body) form what can be called our 'invisible physical body', since at death we leave these three bodies and our physical body in the physical world. Our outer four 'higher' bodies make up our spiritual body that we make use of so we can live in the spiritual world during our physical life and in our life thereafter. Our spiritual body acts as a template for our invisible physical body and our invisible physical body acts as a template for our physical body.

Our auric field carries the energies of our personality, being our emotions, feelings, and thoughts, and is the medium from which our physical body manifests. It works in conjunction with our physical body to facilitate the generation of our emotions, feelings, and thoughts, along with our other combined abilities that we refer to as talents and strengths. During our process of development, our auric field changes as it receives influx from our lower mind. From this relationship we can see that our mind directly influences our mental and physical health.

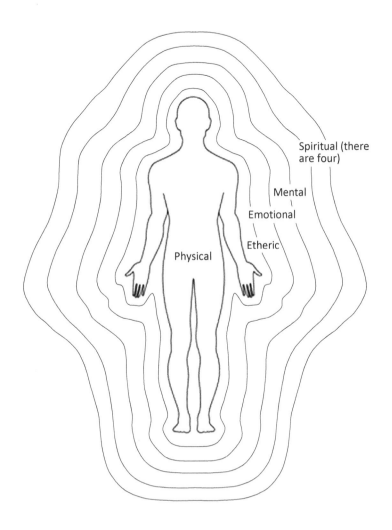

Spiritual (there are four)

Mental

Emotional

Etheric

Physical

Figure 6 Our invisible bodies surrounding our physical body.

> **Our True Self and False Self:**
>
> Our mind uses our spiritual body, 'invisible physical body', brain, and remainder of our physical body for us to have conscious awareness in the physical world. Our personality is the net effect of the influx through our higher mind, lower mind, auric field, and physical body.
>
> It is only when our intention is such that we are drawing from angelic influence through our lower mind that our true self is expressed in our life. Conversely, when our intention is selfish such that we draw from hellish influence through our lower mind, then we express our false or 'monstrous' self.

Working as part of our auric energy system are our chakras. These are rotating energy centres within our energy bodies that transfer energy from our lower mind and the universal energy field to our invisible bodies and then to our physical body. This energy is distributed throughout each of our bodies via a network of nadis/meridians as they are known in Eastern traditions. You may have come across these through complementary health modalities such as acupuncture, reiki, and kinesiology.

Barbara Brennan is a scientist, psychotherapist, healer, and teacher of healing. In her book *Hands of Light,* she explains that we have seven invisible bodies. Our innermost body is Body 1: Etheric and our outermost is Body 7: Higher Mind (Brennan uses the term Divine in place of Higher). Energy from the universal energy field flows into our outermost auric body then into the next inner auric body, etc, until reaching our etheric body, and eventually our physical body.

Each of our invisible bodies works holographically through the other bodies and physical body that they enclose:

- **Body 1: Etheric** – energy movement here correlates to the physical body and our spirit's lower mind's will to live in the physical world. It is the blueprint for our physical body and the source of all physical sensations, painful and pleasurable.

- **Body 2: Emotional** – energy movement here correlates to our spirit's lower mind's emotions and feelings about our self.

- **Body 3: Mental** – energy movement here correlates to the workings of our spirit's lower mind's rational degree and how well it works with our spirit's higher or intuitive mind.

- **Body 4: Relational** (spiritual) – energy movement here correlates with our relationships with others, animals, plants, inanimate objects, earth, sun, stars, and the universe as a whole.

- **Body 5: Higher Intent** (spiritual) – energy movement here correlates with our alignment with Divine intent in our spirit's higher mind manifested into pattern and form. When the body is healthy, we feel great power and connectedness with all that is around us. We will maintain order in our life, be aligned with our purpose, and co-creating with God.

- **Body 6: Higher Love** (spiritual) – energy movement here correlates with our level of Divine Love and affection in our spirit's higher mind. It is our level that corresponds to our experience of faith and hope. When the body is healthy, we commune in love with all lifeforms and experience unconditional love.

- **Body 7: Higher Mind** (spiritual) – energy movement here correlates with our level of Divine Wisdom in our spirit's higher mind. It regulates the flow of energy to and from our auric field. When the body is healthy, we understand and know that we are a part of the great pattern of life, know perfection within our imperfection, and feel safe.

Our energy bodies interact bi-directionally with the energies of our environment. They protect us; filtering out many of the energies we encounter and draw in others that we need. Our higher mind communicates (via our lower mind) through our energy bodies to express our true self. If we are open to this spiritual communication, then we are positive, connected, and on track on our journey towards our spiritual and life goals.

Our fifth auric body, higher intent (will), is a template for our first auric body which contains energy movement correlating to our will to live in the physical world. Our sixth auric body, higher love, is a template for our second auric body which contains energy movement correlating to emotions and feelings about our self. Our seventh auric body, known as higher mind, is a template for our third auric body whose energy movement correlates with our reasoning.

In order for us to become fully self-realised and in harmony with our natural and spiritual nature, we need to harmonise our lowest three auric bodies (having denser energies of lower vibrational frequencies) with the lighter energies of our uppermost three auric bodies (having higher vibrational frequencies). We do this by exercising love in relationships and living our life from good intent by resisting selfish tendencies. This makes use of our fourth auric body which represents the bridge between the physical and spiritual worlds. This has the effect of moving our conscious awareness into our three highest bodies which takes us into the higher aspects of our intent, loves, and reason. In Swedenborg's terms this process takes place as we reform and regenerate when we are growing spiritually. With reformation and regeneration, our intention becomes more courageous, our loves becoming more heavenly, and our reasoning becomes truth. Over time as we consistently continue this transcendental process, our courage becomes more powerful, our love becomes unconditional love, and our truth becomes wisdom.

2.5 Our chakra system and nadis/meridians

As explained previously, chakras are interconnected spiritual energy centres that pass through all our auric bodies. They channel or transmit spiritual energy from our lower mind and from other beings around us both in and out of our auric bodies and physical body. Each chakra transforms and transfers spiritual energy into the vertical power current along the centreline of all our bodies. The energy then flows into bio-energy-circulation pathways (known in Indian traditions as nadis or in Chinese traditions as meridians) in our invisible bodies and physical body, and ultimately to our organs and other body parts that exist throughout all our bodies.

There are seven main chakras (Figure 7 ahead) and many minor chakras such as those in our hands (used by energy healers) and feet that will not be covered in this text. To our spiritual sight, chakras appear as spinning wheel-like vortices of pure energy. In the East they are sometimes referred to as lotus flowers with different numbers of petals. They spin at great speed and in the case of a spiritually developed person, become spheres of intense radiant light energy. Our chakras differ in size and activity in each of us and from person-to-person. They vibrate at different rates relative to our awareness and our ability to integrate the characteristics of each chakra into our life. When we are both balanced and receptive, these energy centres allow our higher mind to be expressed more fully through our personality.

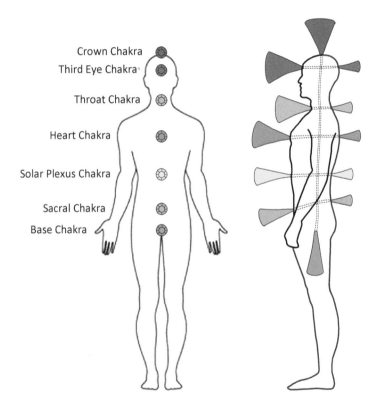

Crown Chakra
Third Eye Chakra
Throat Chakra
Heart Chakra
Solar Plexus Chakra
Sacral Chakra
Base Chakra

Figure 7 The main chakras of our bodies.

Chakra	Location	Colour	Function	Body Parts	When excessive	When blocked	When balanced
Crown	Crown of head	Purple	Spiritual Connection	Muscles, skeleton, nervous system	Spiritual addiction, domination	Depression, disconnect from body	Sees interconnectivity, open-minded
Third Eye	Forehead	Indigo	Mind, intuition, imagination, wisdom	Brain, nervous system, ears, eyes, nose, face	Overly intellectual	Delusions, lack imagination, denial	Innate wisdom and clarity of thought
Throat	Throat	Light blue	Self-expression, communication	Throat, mouth, vocal-chords, thyroid	Overly vocal, poor listener	Fear to speak, shyness	Confident and effective communication
Heart	Heart	Green	Love, forgiveness, relationships	Cardiac system, chest, upper back	Overly emotional, demanding	Withdrawn, shy, depressed	Compassionate, self-love, empathy, peace
Solar Plexus	Solar Plexus	Yellow	Self-esteem, self-worth	Lungs, abdominal organs, lower back	Aggressive, dominating	Lacking drive, low self-esteem	Inner harmony, self-acceptance
Sacral	Lower abdomen	Orange	Sexuality, emotions, creativity	Intestines, pelvis, lymphatic system	Emotional, attachment, addiction	Lack desire and passion	Creative, stable emotionally
Base	Base of spine	Red	Ground spirit to body	Spine, rectum, legs, bones, feet	Sluggish, tiredness, obese	Anger, greed, workaholic	Vitality, grounded, feel safe

Table 1 Chakra characteristics.

We receive and transmit spiritual, mental, emotional, social, sexual, and physical energy through our chakras. Just as every organ in our physical body has its equivalent on all our invisible bodies, every chakra corresponds to specific aspects of our behaviour and development. In general, the front aspects of our second to sixth chakras correlate to our emotional functioning and their rear aspects correlate to our wilfulness function.

Our lower three chakras (base, sacral, and solar plexus) serve our physical body. Together, they are associated with our fundamental intent, emotions, and reason. The energy passing through these chakras vibrates at lower frequencies and is therefore denser in nature. This means that the three work together to influence our self-image and physical and emotional identity, together with our relationship to the physical world. Our middle chakra (heart chakra) serves our emotional connection with other beings. Our upper three chakras (throat, third eye, and crown) serve the higher aspects of our mind. They transmit finer energies and correspond to our higher mental and spiritual aspirations, faculties, and personal and spiritual development.

The actions and energies of all our chakras build one upon each other. If any or all of our lower chakras are significantly blocked, less energy will flow to our higher chakras. We need to raise, balance, and sufficiently clear our three lower chakras to more fully realise our higher mind or true self in our emotions, thoughts, words, and actions. Doing so moves us into higher states of consciousness where we experience greater love, peace, joy, fulfilment, and realisation of what is true and meaningful in our life. We do this by progressively opening our fourth chakra (heart chakra) by becoming more self-aware, compassionate, caring, and applying self-love and acceptance in our life. It is in our heart that we can transcend our ego's false perceptions and judgments to become a more loving, wise, and humble person.

One effect as we grow spiritually is that our heart chakra (and our other chakras) will gradually open. This has the effect of promoting greater energy flow between our upper three chakras and lower three chakras, with this energy being transmitted via our vertical power current along the centreline of our bodies. Ultimately, if we progress to an advanced stage in our spiritual growth, we will reach a major milestone in our development. At this milestone we will experience a shift in our being in that our mind will operate more of the time intuitively rather than rationally. The expression of our love will be driven more from our 'heart' than our 'head'. We will no longer be predominantly making use of our higher mind's spiritual level, but instead now making use of its celestial level. During this time, our heart chakra will make a sudden transition to become much wider opened. This causes a sudden surge of energy through our vertical power current which we will actually feel. Now, our upper three chakras and lower three chakras will work more effectively together, having much greater energy flow between them and throughout our various bodies. As a result of this transformation, we will experience a major shift higher in our level of consciousness. We will then benefit from greater periods of unconditional love, happiness, joy, gratitude, optimism, connectedness with life, peace, forgiveness, and understanding.

When we subject ourselves to negative emotional states of trauma such as shame, fear, or guilt, we do harm to our chakras and invisible bodies of our auric field. These situations can lead to our chakras having unbalanced density, breaks, being under-developed, greatly expanded, distorted, bent to the side, and imbalanced. The effect of these detrimental changes leads to the energy flows through our chakras being adversely affected which means that less energy reaches our body parts. This can result in pain or weakness in the body parts surrounding the chakra(s) and if this occurs for long enough then disease occurs. When we are in balance, we draw abundant energy through our chakras. To be in balance we need to make a habit of avoiding living in negative states such as fear, worry, anxiety, anger, guilt, shame, or apathy. Spiritual growth through self-awareness, understanding, forgiveness, compassion, empathy, concern and caring for others, and resisting selfish desires causes our chakras to heal and open more fully to energy from the Divine.

2.6 Our auric field interactions in relationships

We can best see a reflection of our self through our relationships with others and the world around us. This gives us the opportunity to see the results of our spiritual learnings put into practice and grow from these experiences. We come to see and appreciate God's qualities in our self and others and also those situations when we have turned away from God and suffered from this. The fourth body of our auric field contains the energy correlations to our interactions with the universe: people (and spirits), animals, plants, minerals, the earth, and the rest of the universe. It is in the fourth body of our auric field that we have our energy or 'personality' corresponding to our expression of love for all beings.

Barbara Brennan explains in her book *Light Emerging* that there are three major types of field interactions in the fourth body of our field. Note that these interactions can either be heavenly (for the greater good of all) or hellish (selfish) in nature:

1. *Harmonic induction* of the frequencies of one field into the other person's field. The person with the stronger field will influence the pulsation rates of the other person. When individuals pulse at similar rates, they can communicate more effectively and experience greater pleasure in doing so. Conversely, when frequencies are very different, communication can become difficult. Also, at times we can sense the effect of other people's vibrations entering our auric field. This can be unpleasant when we sense fear, repulsion, dislike, or disgust. At other times we can experience pleasant sensations when we are in harmony with others.

2. *Streamers of bioplasma* flow from person-to-person between their auric fields in an unconscious energy exchange. The energy consciousness in these bioplasmic streamers corresponds with the type of communication taking place between the people involved. Energy exchange can be given mutually, or one person can drain the other of some energy.

3. *Cords of light* from our chakras connect with other's chakras. These cords are grown whenever there is mutual agreement. Cord connections represent a particular aspect of relationship; they can be healthy for interdependent relationships, or unhealthy and entangled for dependent relationships. The fuller and stronger the relationship, the fuller and stronger the cords; and the more interactions, the more cords for that relationship.

3 Spirituality

Spirituality is described in many ways, including living our life so that we allow the Divine to work through us. Spirituality encompasses the life of our mind and most importantly, its development to become more heavenly in nature. When we are well developed spiritually, our higher mind or true self will be expressed more fully in our personality, and we will be more closely following God in our life.

On our spiritual journey we face challenges of various kinds as we live our life, with these challenges giving us the opportunity to see some of our selfish aspects. From these realisations we are able to decide to change our ways by working against our selfishness to heal and grow to ultimately experience the greatest joy and happiness. As this process of growth continues, we become more open to new heavenly ideas, concepts, and ways of living that are aligned with God's will.

3.1 The Divine or God

Swedenborg in his book *True Christian Religion*, describes God or the Divine as the uncreated, unchanging, always was, and always will be from eternity to eternity. God is continuous and infinite in time, space, and power. He is present everywhere, all knowing, Eternal, limitless, boundless - all concepts that our limited human understanding cannot fully comprehend. God is Being itself. God is the source of all things and must sustain all things for them to exist.

Swedenborg explains that God's essence is His Love and Wisdom. God's Divine Love has its end in view to make human beings eternally blessed from His Divine. His Divine Wisdom cannot produce anything but services that are designed to fulfil that end. God is substance itself and form itself, and angels and humans are substances and forms derived from Him; they are images and likenesses of Him to the extent that they are in Him and He in them.

We receive our human (heavenly) qualities from God which He loves to give to us. This allows us to manifest finite facets of His Love as we live. As finite beings, we have a limited ability to fully understand God who is infinite. God sends His Love out to us for us to freely accept into our being, and when we do so we express this love through wisdom in the way we live. As this happens, we unite with Him who in turn nurtures, fulfils, and enriches our life and the lives of others.

3.2 Creation

Swedenborg in his book *Divine Providence*, explains that the Divine or God expresses His fundamental nature of Love in order that the spiritual and physical universes are created, with the ultimate goal to form a Heaven of angels from mankind. His ongoing creative impulse of Love through Wisdom sustains and perpetuates all of creation.

Creation cannot come from nothing; it came and comes from God. What we describe as nothing is the invisible realm of the Divine, full of potentiality. The spiritual and physical universes have been created by God in His image from His spiritual substance being His Love. All creation takes place in the spiritual universe or spiritual world, with its effects being made manifest in the physical universe or physical world. It is an appearance that creation takes place in the physical world.

Since God is uncreated and the physical and spiritual universes are created by God, they cannot be part of God but rather are from God. We too are created both on the spiritual level and the physical level and are not part of God but from God, living in both universes. Being human means that we are able at all times to receive God's Spirit into our being to transform our lives from moment-to-moment. The spiritual and physical universes have no Being of themselves since they are repeatedly being brought into existence in a cyclic process by God. It is this mechanism that allows these universes including us to change.

Part of God's expression of His Love is His ongoing provision of life to the spiritual and physical universes, which of course includes our lives. Likewise, it is only from God's continuous expression of Love that we receive His gift of life which is unconditional (and no true lover ever lays down conditions). He ensures we have freewill throughout our life so we can develop our loving nature, possibly choosing to grow to be angelic in nature - in His image or likeness.

3.3 Our relationship with the Divine

Our senses and proprium (our perception of existing as a separate being, apart from all of creation) 'tell us' that we live from ourselves and that human life is not connected. There comes a time in our lives when we realise that there is more to our existence than what our physical senses tell us. All of us at some point or other have had an inner feeling or experience that there is an invisible world beyond our physical world. This urges us to search deeply within ourselves for the inner truth that we are a spiritual being and that this given life is from God. We come to fully realise this through learning spiritual truths and undertaking spiritual practices on a regular basis, which then allows us to best receive God's subtle communication.

All life originates and is kept in existence by God. We are receptacles or vessels of life from Him. He provides us with all His spiritual nourishment of love and wisdom, goodness and truth, for us to take into our life. All of our being (soul, higher mind, lower mind, auric field, and physical body) is repeatedly brought into existence by God, for He is Eternal and just Is, Being and unchanging. Our life is from Him and is sustained in a cycle of coming into being as we are repeatedly brought to life that continues to eternity. This cycle of coming into existence allows us to change over time.

It is God's nature to give out His Love and Wisdom, so He has created us so we can receive this and grow into more loving and wise human beings. In doing this, we reflect His love out to others and back to Him. When we respond by taking in His heavenly influx of love and wisdom into the way we live, we allow Him to change us for the better into more loving and wise humans. When this takes place, we are growing spiritually. Alternatively, we can reject Him by choosing to be selfish. In this instance His effect will not be manifest in the way we live, and we will become more selfish in our being leading us to destructive emotions, thoughts, words, actions, and separation from Him, others, and all creation.

3.4 Spiritual laws

Swedenborg explains in his book *Divine Providence*, that just as this world operates in accordance with physical and scientific laws that apply consistently and coherently, so there are corresponding spiritual laws which govern all aspects of the spiritual world and our spiritual life. These spiritual laws are in place primarily to provide us with an optimal environment in which to develop spiritually as we choose.

These spiritual laws are:

- **Divine Providence** in action, which has for its end the utmost eternal happiness of every person.
- **Freewill** which allows us to develop our loving spiritual nature, since love can only exist in freedom.

Divine Providence and freewill work together to ensure that we always have the utmost beneficial influence from God to counteract the opposing negative influence from the hells.

Swedenborg explains that it is an appearance that our life is very much our own. He challenges us to embrace the reality that God is Life itself and we are but recipients of His life. Our lives are not our own, but the ways in which we respond as receivers of life are our own. It is through God's Love and Wisdom that we have been given the power to progressively choose the ongoing development of our spirit. Most importantly, our lives fail to bear heavenly fruit in our spirit until we act by the good we know.

3.5 Divine Providence

All of us are blessed to be given a perfect spiritual environment at all times to allow us to be gifted with Divine qualities. These heavenly qualities are experienced with far greater power should we pass on to become angels in heaven after we die. It is God's Divine Providence which provides such an environment as will now be covered.

Swedenborg explains in his book *Divine Providence* that Divine Providence is the foreseeing protection and care of all

God's creatures in all areas of life enacted through Divine Love and Wisdom at all times. He states that God's Providence has for its ultimate goal a heaven of angels from the human race. As this is the goal, then Providence looks to what is best eternally in the lives of all. Whilst circumstances and events have an influence on our lives, God always uses our everyday happenings and events to lead us towards a loving relationship with Him and others, and a life of heavenly use. Because God is all knowing from eternity to eternity, He is able to provide us with the perfect heavenly influx for us moment-by-moment during our life, so we have the opportunity to make the best possible choices for our spiritual welfare and physical life.

The operation of Providence to lead us to heaven governs our lives at all times of our physical existence. Importantly, Providence is working in unseen and unfelt ways to ensure our freewill is always maintained to promote our ultimate growth for our eternal welfare. Freewill is essential for spiritual growth for it allows us to turn away from our selfish desires by choosing good actions. It also allows us to receive God's Love and Wisdom and Goodness and Truth into our being.

We can sometimes see the after-effects of Providence when we look back on our life at the loving coincidences, synchronicities, and situations that we have benefited from. Seeing Providence in this way gives us the confidence and trust to know that we are being led in the present even if we cannot see this happening in the moment. There are far too many coincidences and synchronicities with enormous odds of occurrence for them to really be simply chance. Instead, we are recognising those most obvious occasions when

God's continuous leading has taken place - although the leading is actually taking place all the time.

We can sometimes doubt God's workings, saying to ourselves "If God is a god of love, why does He allow bad things to happen?" This question is inferring that God is in all disasters and evil which cannot be further from the truth. It is not that God is causing bad outcomes to happen. God has provided us with all the resources with which to live happy and healthy lives. However, all of us at various times of our lives have chosen to turn away from God and in doing so we and other people have suffered. Also, we can't possibly fully comprehend the spiritual significance of events. The events that we may perceive as bad are most certainly governed by Providence to bring about the greatest good to eternity while ensuring we have the freedom to choose our destiny.

There are many circumstances where if God were to intervene against disaster then His perfect natural system would be out of order. Earthquakes and extreme weather events occur because it is part of the order of creation and God cannot act outside His order. In many parts of the world we have increased the risk of harm to ourselves by for example, living in unwise ways in regions that are prone to natural disasters.

It is also important that we recognise God's Providence is universal - His leading is constantly being offered to those who tend towards good and also to those who tend towards evil. Unfortunately for those who tend towards evil, they often respond to situations in ways such that His influence is rejected, and instead negative, harmful influence is accepted and acted upon resulting in destructive outcomes.

3.6 Freewill

What is Freewill?

As the highest form in creation, we have the ability to grow spirituality. This means we have freewill to develop a loving relationship with God and with other people as we choose by aiming to do what we believe is best for the good of all. Alternatively, we can decide to satisfy ourselves with complete disregard for our effect on others, and in doing so turn away from living a life following God.

How does Freewill Operate?

The life-sustaining energy and substance that flows into us from God is love and wisdom. If we embrace this love and wisdom and try to listen for the gentle voice of conscience that it produces, it will provide the loving thoughts and inclinations that enable us to love others and embody good ideas. These good influences are our heavenly influx. If heavenly influx were our only influence, we would be nothing more than vessels for God's love where goodness and truth is imposed on us. Our affections and thoughts would be handed to us and we would not be free to think or act. We would be nothing more than organisms that perform 'good' actions.

Swedenborg writes in Divine Providence, that in order for us to be human, it is absolutely necessary that we have the opportunity to develop our loving nature. For this to happen, God ensures we experience freewill throughout our life. He does this by continuously providing us with a proportion of heavenly influx that counterbalances the hellish influx we are exposed to. As such, we are constantly choosing to draw either heavenly or hellish influx into our being from moment-to-moment and in doing so we act on it.

God allows hell to reach into our lives and influence us (hellish influx), just as His heavenly influx influences us. Swedenborg explains that hellish influx comprises hellish love (selfish love) and foolishness. He notes that God gives us the ability to love hell through all the ways we can love ourselves, such as thinking we are above all others, satisfying ourselves ahead of everyone else, and thinking we deserve more than others. By allowing us to suffer from our own and other people's selfish decisions and actions, Swedenborg explains that God gives us the tools to recognise this behaviour as evil and destructive. In this way, God gives us freedom to choose between good and evil and make our own decisions.

While God provides all good things through heaven, hell provides us with influx to selfishly love ourselves and worldly things (greedily gathering material possessions and wanting others to serve us) and to reject all good things and love evil. These two opposing influences give us two paths to choose between, and those choices over time form our character. Through our intention, God's love meets the influence of hellish love. Moment-by-moment, we have the freedom for our love to be directed to the greatest good for all or to suit just ourselves - which Swedenborg states are opposites.

Hellish influx supplies us with everything we need to connect with hell to be selfish, destructive, and separate ourselves from God and others. Whenever we are struggling with selfish impulses or negative emotions, feelings, thoughts and actions, heavenly influx allows for Divine love and good influences to flow in and provide support. If we go through life searching for the good and God's love, Swedenborg states that God will continue to open our minds and allow us to receive more of His Love and Wisdom.

> **Negative thoughts don't always harm us:**
> Note that experiencing negative thoughts won't harm us spiritually provided the motivation behind our thoughts is from goodness. It's only when we experience negative thoughts while having selfish motives that we are harming ourselves spiritually.

Swedenborg explains we all need freedom from a balance of heavenly and hellish influx to be able to think and act for ourselves. That is the only way that human beings are able to love God from their own 'hearts and minds'. This leads to an apparently contradictory yet key principle of Swedenborg's theology.

> *The only way we can <u>freely</u> choose to follow God is if He allows us to leave Him.*

Swedenborg explains in his book *Divine Love and Wisdom* that there are three key principles relating to spiritual growth:

- Firstly, we can only see evils from good (God in us), but we cannot see good from evil. Evil motives are justified by falsity. Falsity cannot see truth since it is clouded in illusion. Also, evil cannot be objective since it is only concerned with its own self-interest.
- Secondly, we must be in freedom in order for us to restrain ourselves from evils.

- Thirdly, our will in our lower mind is our organ for heavenly love to act through. For heavenly love to enter our will, it must be through our love or affection for something. It is only by being subjected to freewill that we can act from love or affection and take any goodness and truth into our lower mind's will and understanding to grow spiritually.

Therefore, we have freedom in order that we may be affected by goodness in love and truth in wisdom, and love truth. God is then able to implant His goodness and truth in our spirit for us to use in our life – it is not ours but belongs to God.

> *For we cannot receive God's love and return it to Him unless we feel it is ours to give.*

We receive life from God, feeling that this life is from ourselves, even though it is God powering us at all times. It is necessary for us to feel as if our life is from ourselves so that we may receive God's goodness and truth into our higher mind and lower mind and grow spiritually.

Origin of freewill

Freewill originates from the effect of angels and evil spirits with us in the spiritual world, where our spirit (containing our mind) is kept by God. The spiritual world is made up of heaven, the intermediate realm or world of spirits, and hell. Heaven lies 'overhead' of the intermediate realm where our spirits dwell (while we live in the physical world), and hell lies 'beneath' that realm. The intermediate realm appears as an entire world. Our spirits are kept in a middle state between heaven and hell by the influences of the angels and evil spirits with us and thereby in spiritual equilibrium where we have freewill.

3.7 Faith

Many of us think of faith as being a conviction or belief, or knowledge of something. This type of faith is known as natural faith when it is devoid of spiritual essence, being heavenly love. Whereas spiritual faith, or faith, is an internal acknowledgement of truth from our higher mind (with the truth being loved). In other words, we have developed a love for that truth so that intuitively we know the truth without needing to rationally think it through. For example, we might learn that it is good to treat others as we would like to be treated. Initially this knowledge is in our memory only, being natural faith. Over time as we practice this truth, we develop a love to treat others as we would like to be treated. This truth then becomes faith as we no longer need to think about it and instead we know it and act on it intuitively.

Faith is an ultimate knowing based on truth that is derived through our higher intuition. It involves influx from our higher mind entering our lower mind to give us a direct knowing of truth. During this process, the influx from our higher mind flows more fully through our lower mind with less restriction and distortion and is enhanced by angelic influence in our lower mind. It then flows from our lower mind through our auric field and into our physical body. In this process we perceive a finite aspect of overall reality which Swedenborg refers to as perception. Our perception varies with our state of spiritual development which is in line with our state of consciousness or awareness of Life from the Divine (explained in chapter 6).

When we are living through faith, which is not the operation of rationalising our thoughts using the rational part of our mind, we connect our lower mind to our higher mind (our true self). This sets, balances, and charges our auric field into a healing state. We have our energy bodies in our auric field operating in greater harmony and synchronicity. Our energetic system is enhanced, and we are in greater spiritual and physical health. We are then following God. Our whole being is in greater alignment with the Divine and we are more fully acting as a vessel for God to work through us in our life. As such we have greater heavenly impact in our day-to-day life.

God's leading and faith work hand-in-hand. Whenever we act with courage to overcome our fears by exercising faith, we follow God's leading. And as we follow God's leading, our faith grows as we learn truths and live by them, progressing along our spiritual journey. Importantly, when we act from faith we are acting with goodness. In this instance we are not living from our proprium or self-centredness. We are allowing God to lead us so that we express heavenly power in our life through wisdom. The more we follow God, the more spiritual power we exercise to carry out our true life purpose.

Swedenborg explains in his book *True Christian Religion* that faith is a link with God by means of truths in our understanding and thus to thought. We are also linked with God by means of various kinds of good in our will and thus to our love (expressed as emotions) and affections (expressed as feelings being finer components of an emotion). Our will seeks means and ways of achieving its purpose by working through our understanding. Our understanding directs our will to result in our good actions. From this it follows that our good deeds or use in *essence* belong to our will, in *form* to our understanding, and in *performance* to our body. This is how charity (which is having good will) working with our faith (groupings of truth that are loved) becomes a good deed. A truly good deed is doing good driven from our will as we acknowledge God working through us and not done thinking it is from our own source or power. It is always God that is the source and power behind our good deeds. Most importantly, charity and faith are merely mental concepts until they come into existence together when realised in deeds. When this occurs, a person does the deeds intelligently and wisely.

3.8 Temptations

When there is difference between the focus of our higher mind and our lower mind, we experience conflict in the form of temptations - our struggle to make our lower mind submit to our higher mind. Our lower mind is the only part of our mind that can be out of Divine order, cause us problems, and be corrupted. It is our lower mind that exercises freewill, and it is there that we choose either to obey or disobey God's commandments. When we choose self-compelled obedience, our lower mind is aligned with our higher mind and goodness results in our actions.

Temptations are explained in greater detail in section 5.3.

3.9 Rebirth and spiritual growth

In order for us to progress spiritually and move toward a more heavenly nature, our lower mind needs to be reformed and regenerated (part of the spiritual growth process). Swedenborg explains this is what is meant by John 3:3: "Most assuredly, I say to you, unless one is born again, he cannot see the kingdom of God." When we make a committed change from living a life dominated by selfishness towards living a life dominated by goodness, we are said to be reborn. Note that being reborn is just the beginning. To develop a predominantly angelic nature, spiritual growth needs to be a regular and ongoing process throughout our life.

For reformation and regeneration to happen, our higher mind must take possession of and transform our lower mind. Initially, we need to recognise some of our selfishness, and acknowledge how it adversely impacts others and the world around us. Then we need to adopt a change in attitude towards greater goodness in our life. This stage in the spiritual growth process is known as repentance. Then we must resist our selfish desires, thoughts, and actions (temptations) because they take us away from God's love and not because we wish to look good in front of others or appear to be doing the right thing so that we might gain from such action in the future. As we resist our selfishness, we make 'room' in our mind for God's love and wisdom, goodness and truth to be implanted.

In the beginning of our life we are all born with a corrupt and under-developed lower mind. During adolescence, many of us are often overly self-centred in our outlook. To be reborn we must experience a change in our outlook to being less self-centred. We need to live according to God's love and truth, motivated by real goodness. Whenever our actions are motivated by spiritual love (love to others), the spiritual level of our higher mind will open more. As this happens, what exists at the spiritual level (love to others) of our higher mind will flow down into our lower mind (containing our will and understanding) and make it more spiritual in quality.

The celestial level is 'above' the spiritual level of our higher mind. For us to draw upon the celestial level of our higher mind we need to live by loving God. We love God by obeying His commandments because we love Him and want to serve Him best, and in doing so serve the greater good of all. When we love Him, we allow His love to flow from the celestial level (love to God) of our higher mind down into our lower mind and we experience heavenly love in our life. As this happens our lower mind becomes more celestial in quality.

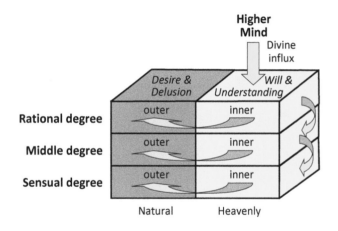

Figure 8 Implanting of heavenly qualities in our lower mind.

This process where our higher mind reforms and regenerates our lower mind takes place in several ways as shown in Figure 8. Our higher mind gradually reforms and regenerates the rational degree of our lower mind so that our rational degree more so serves our higher mind. As this happens, our rational degree gradually reforms and regenerates our middle degree so that our middle degree more so serves our rational degree. Simultaneously and finally, our middle degree gradually reforms and regenerates our sensual degree so that our sensual degree more so serves our middle degree.

Reformation and regeneration of our lower mind is broken down even further as spiritual growth takes place within each degree (rational, middle, and sensual). Each degree's inner heavenly part where our will and understanding reside, develops its outer natural part where our desire and delusion reside. Now we are more reformed and regenerated on all degrees. The end result is that both our higher mind and lower mind have become transformed and more developed spiritually, and we have become more loving and wise.

Spiritual growth is explained in greater detail in section 5.3.

4 Divine Love, Wisdom and the Human

Divine Love or heavenly love is the ultimate powerful energy and substance which creates all things and flows and connects everything in the spiritual and physical universes. This love flows into us and is expressed from us towards God, others, and all life in emotions, feelings, thoughts, ideas, and actions that are directed toward a common good for all without selfish intent. Divine Wisdom is the ultimate powerful and all-knowing understanding and intelligence that directs all of creation for the greater good of all beings.

4.1 Love and Wisdom

When we think of love we should think of motivation, use, caring, compassion, and the courage to act for the greatest benefit to all persons and life concerned, according to what we believe to be true and right. In a heavenly state of love, we love what is good, honest, and fair because it is good, honest, and fair, and we perform uses because of that love. When we love these things for their own sake and act from this love, we also love God supremely, because these things come from Him.

Love of God conjoins or unites us with Him. Love of others conjoins or unites us with those we have affection for and are connecting with. This occurs with those of us in this world and also with those who have passed into the spiritual world. As Swedenborg explains, this is how it operates in the spiritual world; spirits are instantly present with the spirits they love or desire to be with. On the other hand, the opposite is also true, because hate creates its own distance and separation. It creates a great gulf between people and spirits.

> **Two paradoxes of heavenly love:**
>
> 1. Love increases in giving; we become a more loving person and we give others the opportunity to receive this love and become more loving too.
> 2. The more we love a person or God, the more free, individual, and independent we become, and our personality becomes more energised; this happens because we live more so from a state of courage and less and less from a state of fear.

Love in personal relationships makes each person's personality shine with greater brightness. This is because to love is to set others free – never to see them as a possession, never to try to mould them into a likeness of you or control them, because you love their uniqueness, their unknown depths and wonderful characteristics. You and your partner, child, or friend are 'distinctly one' since all of us are able to draw in a unique way from God's infinite qualities and live them in our being. It is our distinction that creates the joy, playfulness, and undiscovered potential ever fresh in us. Note that the speed of love is immediate and reaches those we love in the instant that we express it. It works this way in the spiritual world where time and space are experienced differently to the physical world.

During times when we are displaying the highest expression of love, it can only ever be a likeness of God's perfect love – of course never reaching His love. Genuine love desires the good of all, seeks to impart to all everything it can of itself, and seeks to give to others all that is its own. For Swedenborg, genuine love seeks to share all that is good, wise, or delightful with others. This involves participating with others in shared life. Genuine love also involves empathically and compassionately responding to the suffering of others as if toward our own. Love is the motivation behind our whole life. Ultimately, our emotions, feelings, thoughts, and actions are a result of our motivating love (heavenly or hellish) guided by our understanding or delusion. We need to pay attention to the quality of our love since it determines our connections. We need to see ourselves as being connected to all of God's creation which supports a love for each and all beings and all of creation.

> **Love and wisdom in angels:**
> Swedenborg, *Divine Love and Wisdom*
> The likeness and image of God appear clearly in angels, for love from within them shines forth in their faces, and wisdom in their beauty - the form of their love.

We all continuously receive the Divine Life of Love and Wisdom working together enabling us to live as feeling and thinking beings. Heavenly love does not exist in isolation but is given in freedom to people and creation to serve good and useful purposes. God's love toward us is not always understood since He is constantly directing his energies towards our spiritual growth – something which means challenges and difficulties for us at various times to enable us to become aware of our selfishness, develop, and grow.

Divine Love, Wisdom, and Use

In his book *Divine Love and Wisdom*, Swedenborg explains that love is the source of all that is created. God is Love itself. God is also Wisdom itself. Life from the Divine Itself being Consciousness, comprises the unity of Love (the energy and substance of life) and Wisdom (manifestation of life – love's quality). While the intellectual mind sees them as distinct, Swedenborg explains that in reality one does not exist without the other.

Love and Wisdom are united:

Swedenborg, *Divine Love and Wisdom*

Even though love and wisdom are two distinct things, they are united or bound together because love motivates wisdom, and wisdom is the means to express love.

Love, Wisdom, and Use – a fundamental trinity:

Swedenborg, *Conjugial Love*

Love united with Wisdom is not static but necessarily looks to and generates a third aspect, the *Use* it can be to creation. Thus, there exists this fundamental trinity in unity.

Without use, love and wisdom are merely abstract ideas of thought...but in use, the two are brought together and become a one which is real.

"Because God is Love itself and Wisdom itself, He is also Use itself. For love has use for its end and brings forth use by means of wisdom."

God's Love and Wisdom never occur without each other, and they proceed together into action, power, or uses. God's Love, Wisdom, and Action or Use always proceed and govern as one. For example, caring for a child has love of the child as the motivation, knowledge of how to care for the child acted through wisdom, and the wellbeing of the child as the good use. Love must have a use to perform, for that use is loved. Wisdom must be driven by love for any use to eventuate. Therefore, a use must be loved and facilitated by wisdom for something real to be created. As such, use is the result of wisdom and love. Love without use is an abstract entity and therefore not real love at all.

This means that we really are only truly loving when we are motivated to perform good uses and acting through wisdom (related groupings of truth that we have a love for). When we act through wisdom, we are applying wisdom in our being to the act at hand to perform good uses. This means we are intuitively performing good uses because we love to do these things.

Love→Affections→Intentions→Perceptions→Thoughts→Ideas
Swedenborg, *Divine Love and Wisdom*

Love in our will (which we experience as emotion) is comprised of many various affections being goodness (that we experience as feelings). Our affections generate intentions for good use that flow into our understanding. Our intentions drive our understanding which perceives and produces thoughts then memories and ideas. These affections, intentions, thoughts, and ideas together direct our speech and other physical actions.

Swedenborg explains that true wisdom is very different to what many people understand wisdom to be. He says that the power to grow wise is not the power to reason about spiritual matters from a person's knowledge, but to discern what is true and good from perception or intuition (without reasoning) and apply this for use in their life. Growing wise means that we are evermore able to act in loving ways in our life and with greater depth of love behind the 'actions'. These 'actions' can be in either thought, feelings, speech, or physical activities.

It is important to realise that intelligence is often misunderstood in many societies around the world. Some people think intelligence is the ability to be clever, however, this is a limited interpretation of true intelligence. Swedenborg explains that true intelligence is when a person is being smart motivated by goodness and that cunning is when a person is being smart motivated by selfishness or evil.

4.2 Goodness and Truth

Swedenborg explains in his books *Conjugial Love* and *Divine Love and Wisdom,* that heavenly love is a spiritual energy and substance in our higher mind and in our will in our lower mind. Heavenly love consists of many varied and related affections or goodness in a hierarchy. Heavenly love (or on a finer scale goodness) is the motivating energy to perform beneficial actions in life. Wisdom is a spiritual substance in our higher mind and in our understanding in our lower mind. Wisdom consists of many varied truths that are ordered and related. Truth is the mechanism to create form or good deeds and the quality of life. Form or good use comes about as love (or on a finer scale goodness) provides the motivating energy and substance, while wisdom (or on a finer scale, truth) directs the shape or form (good deed) that manifests. Good use or creation can only come about as love motivates wisdom or goodness motivates truth.

When we are performing good deeds, we allow goodness in our will to provide the motivating spiritual energy and substance for truth in our understanding to direct the form that goodness takes and become visible. This means that our actions are motivated by goodness in our will and directed by truth in our understanding. Truth is the means or mechanism to manifest good deeds or good use. Some goodness is instilled in us in our early life in the form of what Swedenborg calls remains. However, truth is not born in us and must be learnt and then thought about or rationalised and lived for it to be united with goodness. There is life or energy and substance in goodness but no life in truth. Goodness flows into truth providing it with the energy and substance for form or good deeds to be realised.

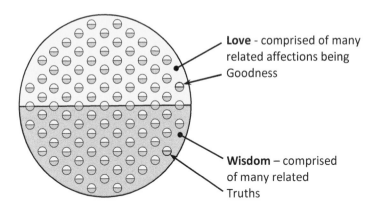

Love - comprised of many related affections being Goodness

Wisdom – comprised of many related Truths

Figure 9 Love united with Wisdom, Goodness united with Truth.

During spiritual growth, we first learn truths, rationalise them, and apply them in our life through our understanding of what are good acts, and in doing so we perform good uses. At this stage in our spiritual growth cycle we are not motivated by a love for this truth but by a different love that is not directly associated with this truth. Swedenborg refers to this as "goodness from truth" in that we perform good deeds as a result of rationalising this truth during our actions. As we continue to perform good deeds, we rationalise less and less as our love for living this truth through the action of the deeds increases. In essence, we develop a love for applying these truths. Eventually we perform these good uses from our love for these uses which Swedenborg refers to as "truth from goodness." Our love of this truth (goodness) is driving our deeds and our truths are made truer and built upon further in the process. Now we are doing our good deeds intuitively and we have become more loving and wise.

4.3 Heavenly loves vs. hellish loves

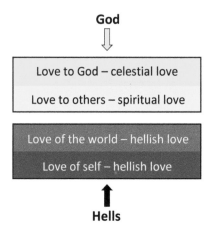

Figure 10 Our four types of love.

In his book *Divine Love and Wisdom*, Swedenborg explains that the love we take into our being can come from four different types of loves as shown in Figure 10. Gaining an understanding of these different types of love helps us to evaluate when we are being motivated from goodness or selfishness, and therefore when we are on-track or off-track in our lives. When we exercise our upper two loves, we allow God to work through us in our life. This further opens and develops these aspects of heavenly love in our higher mind and heavenly part of our lower mind (our will). Swedenborg refers to love to God in a person as being a likeness of Divine Love, and he refers to love to others in a person as being an image of Divine Love.

If our predominant love is towards God (we follow His commandments ahead of the promptings from our ego) then we are in love to God. If our predominant love is towards other people, then Swedenborg refers to this as charity or spiritual love. If we have lived our lives predominantly being in love to God or love towards others, then we will have developed a heavenly loving nature with associated wisdom. When we pass into the spiritual world, we will come into heaven, and like other angels, we will be wise in things that we were unaware of while we lived in the physical world.

The lower two hellish loves are purely selfish and reign in hell. Hellish loves are the desire to satisfy our self with no regard for God, others, or creation. Whereas heavenly loves consist of many varied and related affections being goodness, hellish loves consist of many varied and related evils. Love of the world is the motivation to be served by others and gain materially in our life. Love of self is a motivation to benefit our self with total disregard for others. Love of self is the exact opposite of love to God and love of the world is the exact opposite of love to others. While heavenly love is united with wisdom, hellish love is united with foolishness. When these two hellish loves that are the source of everything evil and false are in control, they restrict influx from our higher mind, corrupt our lower mind, auric field, and physical body.

Even though all of us are created for heaven, Swedenborg explains that we inherit selfish loves from our ancestors. This means we are born with selfish loves resident in our lower mind that we sometimes add to, draw upon, and strengthen during our life. When we selfishly love our self and act in selfish ways to gain materialistically, we fail to apply spiritual truths in our life. In all cases, selfishness stems from false beliefs fuelled by various fears. For example, we may deceive others to gain from them because we fear that our needs will not be met if we do the right thing by them. Or our fear of not getting what we want may lead us to become angry with others in order to get what we want. In any case, when our actions come from a selfish motivation based on fear, we are being destructive, and we drive our self away from others, creation, and God.

Love to God - Heavenly

God's Love is unconditional, universal to all of creation, and aimed at the greatest good for all. When we are exercising love to God (celestial love), we are loving the good that comes from Him by directing it through our lives. We act on our love to God when through wisdom we manifest good use. In this case our love to God is motivating us to perform good deeds in our life. This makes use of our celestial conscience. Merely knowing what is good and true, and understanding this or speaking of this, is not loving God. It is only when we exercise our love in practice (through wisdom and use) that we actually love God. When we exercise love to God from our heart, we allow Him to flow through our being and we become a likeness of Him.

In his book *Secrets of Heaven*, Swedenborg explains that love to God is based on our personal relationship of devotion to Him, which means we strive to learn His truths to apply in our life in accordance with His Commandments. Loving God takes place through the practice of goodness and truth in our life – we love what is good, honest, and fair for its own sake, and act on this motivation through our understanding of what is truth or the right thing to do.

> **Conjunction with God:**
>
> Swedenborg, *Divine Love and Wisdom*
>
> It is not possible for God to be in any angel or human unless they perceive and feel God's Love and Wisdom as if it is theirs. By this God is not only received, but having been received is retained, and also loved in return. This is the reason we must be kept in a state of freewill so that it is possible for conjunction or union to take place. For love can only exist in freedom.

God's love is directed towards the whole human race. He wishes to bring everyone to heaven to share His love. When we have love to God, we also possess finite aspects of His love, and because of this we cannot help loving others. Therefore, love to God embraces love to others. When we are in love to God, we open our higher mind more. This allows a greater amount and quality of Divine influx to flow into our lower mind, enhancing it with more goodness and truth, and improving our auric field and physical health.

Love to Others - Heavenly

Swedenborg explains in his book *New Jerusalem and Its Heavenly Doctrine,* and also in his book *Secrets of Heaven,* that loving others means to love the heavenly qualities in the person, being goodness and truth. It is to seek to support and bring out the best in others according to our conscience. When we are in love to others, we open our higher mind more. This allows a greater amount and quality of influx from our higher mind to flow into our lower mind, enhancing our lower mind with more goodness and truth. Our auric field also benefits along with our physical body.

Charity or Love to Others:

Swedenborg, *New Jerusalem and Its Heavenly Doctrine*

Charity or love to others, is to act prudently and for the sake of the end, that good may result to others. When we exercise love to others, we allow God to work through us, which makes us an image of God. An image is not a likeness but approaches a likeness.

Charity exists whenever we sincerely seek goodness towards others. And this may involve assertive action, and also denial and refusal if these are thought to be in the best interests of another.

Love to others is not something which is exercised towards just a few people such as those whom we know and like. It is to be exercised towards everyone, even though the way in which we apply it will vary considerably depending on the situation. For example, for some people and situations we will need to show affection and give praise. On other occasions we might need to be assertive in order that good outcomes take place. What matters most is that we love and foster the good or heavenly qualities in another whether we like them or not.

There are, as Swedenborg points out, variations of others. Others can also be thought of collectively. The community, for example, is others in a wider sense than a single individual, and our country and world is others in a wider sense still. How best, you may ask, do I serve others, my community, country, and the world? The ways are numerous, but one of the most important ways is the primary role or work we do. If we do that well, we may well do more for the common good than in many other ways.

Love of the World - Hellish

Swedenborg refers to a selfish motivation to be served by others and gain materially as love of the world. This type of love restricts and distorts some of the influx flowing from our higher mind through our lower mind. As a result, some of the goodness and truth from our higher mind is turned into evil and falsity. This corrupts our lower mind with more evil and falsity and is detrimental to our auric field and physical body.

In his book *Secrets of Heaven*, Swedenborg explains that love of the world desires pleasure and ease through being served by others and by acquiring material goods from others. This includes love of wealth as a means of advancement to honours, the love of honours and distinctions as a means to acquiring wealth, and the love of wealth simply for the sake of wealth. We are in the love of the world when we regard and pursue nothing but gain in what we think and do, regardless whether this is acquired to the detriment of others.

When we are in evil from love of the world, we regard others mainly on account of their wealth, not themselves. We desire to gain the most we can when we can from others, and when we are in this form of greed, we are then without charity and mercy; for to gain from others is the delight of our life. We have a selfish concern for our self without regard to God, others, life, and everything, resulting in destructive activities.

Love of Self - Hellish

Love of self is based on motivation where we aim to benefit only our self and not others. Others can benefit as a by-product, although this was not our intention. Love of self is also being 'good' to others only for the sake of our own reputation, advancement, or praise; so that unless we see some such reward in the 'good' we may do for them, we say at heart, "What's the use? Why should I? What's in it for me?" and if we fail to see any self-benefit, we forget about it. This shows that when we are caught up in love of self, we are not loving others, our community, or anything worthwhile—only ourselves. When we are caught up in love of self, we do not intentionally serve our community or fellow citizens. We want our fellow-citizens and communities to serve us and we do not want to serve them. We place our self above them, and them beneath us. Love of self takes away from others and robs others of delight, directing it to itself - for it wishes well to itself alone.

In his book *Secrets of Heaven*, Swedenborg explains that the evils from love of self are the worst of all. The effects of being in this type of love is that the flow of influx from our higher mind to our lower mind is more restricted. Also, some of the good and truth from our higher mind is turned into evil and falsity. This corrupts our lower mind with more evil and falsity and is detrimental to our auric field and physical body. Swedenborg explains that we are caught up in love of self whenever we fail to consider others in what we are thinking and doing, and therefore we give no consideration to the public welfare, let alone God. We are conscious only of ourselves and our immediate circle who are 'ours' or who serve us. This means that when we do something for the sake of ourselves and our immediate circle and it does benefit the public or others, it is by chance or for the sake of appearances.

In referring to "ourselves and our immediate circle," is meant that when we love ourselves, we also love those we claim as our own because we see them as serving us or as a reflection or derivation of us and don't see them in their own right. These people can be our children and grandchildren whereby we are loving what we see as our self in them. Included in those we call "ours" is everyone who praises us, respects us, sides with us, and reveres us. People in the love of self, despise all others in comparison with themselves who do not stand with them or serve them. We are caught up in love of self when we regard anyone who disagrees with us as an enemy - anyone who does not respect and revere us, and we belittle them because of this. We are still more deeply caught up in love of self if for such reasons we harbor hatred toward others and persecute them, and even more deeply if we burn with vengeance toward them and crave their destruction. People who do this come to delight in revenge and cruelty.

Furthermore, to the extent that its reins are loosened (that is, with the removal of the outward restraints exerted by fear of the law and its penalties, and by fear of losing reputation, respect, profit, office, and life), Swedenborg states that love of self by its very nature goes so wild that it wants to rule not only over every country on earth but even over heaven and over the Divine itself. It knows no boundary or limit. This is the hidden agenda of all who are caught up in love of self, even though it may not be so evident in the physical world where the outward reins and restraints keep it in check. When people like this find themselves blocked, they bide their time until an opportunity to exercise this love occurs. Unfortunately, when we are caught up and fixated in this love, we fail to realise that this kind of utterly senseless craving lies hidden within us and is driving our destructive emotions, feelings, thoughts, and actions.

Swedenborg writes on love of self:

Swedenborg, *New Jerusalem and Its Heavenly Doctrine*

The evils belonging to those who are in the love of self are in general; contempt of others, envy, enmity against those by whom they are not favoured, and hostile actions on this ground. Also, hatreds of various kinds, revenges, cunning, deceit, mercilessness, and cruelty.

4.4 Our ruling love

Throughout our life in this world we are continually making choices which contribute to who we become – a person who serves the good of the whole, or a person who lives self-centredly and loves to dominate, control, or gain from others. We come to identify either with the selfless life which is lived in heaven or with the selfish life which is lived in hell. As a result of the countless choices we make during our physical life, we form a dominant focus for our life - our ruling love. For example, if we love wealth more than anything else, whether in the form of money or in the form of possessions, we are constantly calculating how we can acquire it. We feel the deepest pleasure when we do acquire it and the deepest grief when we lose it—our heart is in it. However, if we love caring for children more than anything else, we often think loving thoughts of and care for children we encounter. We gain the greatest joy when we are able to love and care for children.

We all have a unique set of motivations or loves that determines our heaven if we are good and our hell if we are evil. It is what we essentially will or desire to do, everything we claim to be, and our nature. It is what influences us in our life and doesn't change after death since it is what motivates us above all - and we wouldn't want that to change. Everything we find pleasing, satisfying, and happy comes to us from our many loves and ultimately our ruling love. We call whatever we love pleasing because that is how it feels to us. Basically, the things that we experience and enjoy we see as good in our mind and those things we do not enjoy we see as bad in our mind.

In his book *New Jerusalem and Its Heavenly Doctrine*, Swedenborg explains that our life is primarily motivated by our greatest love and reflected in our thoughts. Our greatest love, known as our ruling love, is in our will if we are predominantly heavenly in nature, or in our desire if we are predominantly selfish in nature. Our ruling love is what animates us overall. It has many loves subordinate to it, loves that derive from it. They take on various appearances, but nevertheless these specific loves are inherent in our ruling love and together with it make a single domain. Our ruling love is like their monarch or head, with our specific loves answering to our ruling love. It governs them and works through them as intermediate goals, in order to focus on and strive for its own goal, the primary and ultimate of all. It does this both directly and indirectly.

Swedenborg explains that by the time of our death, our overall pattern of love (with its ruling love) will be set and will no longer be able to change. If our ruling love is heavenly, then we will pass on to live in the spiritual world as an angel in a heavenly society that has the same ruling love. If our ruling love is hellish, we will pass on to live in the spiritual world as an evil spirit in a hellish society that has the same ruling love. To repeat the point, it is only during our life in the physical world that our ruling love can change while we experience freewill and develop spiritually.

4.5 Male and female spiritual makeup

We all know that males and females are very different in nature. However, many of us do not know that these differences come about from the different spiritual makeup of male and female minds. A male's way of being is expressed more from his 'head' whereas a female's way of being is expressed more from her 'heart'.

Swedenborg explains in his book *Conjugial Love* that our mind is created, develops, and exists in the spiritual world and is made of spiritual substance being goodness and truths and evils and falsities. Goodness and truths are positive substances that enter the heavenly part of our human mind – our higher mind and heavenly part of our lower mind; however, evils and falsities are negative substances that enter the outer natural part of our lower mind.

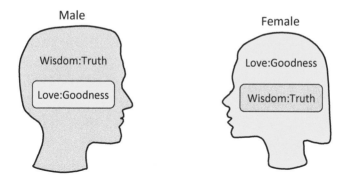

Figure 11 Our spiritual composition: heavenly part of our minds.

Both male and female minds are constituted of the same spiritual substances from the spiritual world: goodness and truths; and evils and falsities. However, there is a difference in the organisation of these spiritual substances within male and female minds. Within the heavenly part of male and female minds, goodness and truths vary in terms of their externality or internality as can be seen in Figure 11.

For a male, the heavenly part of their mind has inner love or goodness and external wisdom or truth. For a female, the heavenly part of their mind has inner wisdom or truth covered over with external love or goodness. What this means is that as far as the heavenly part of our mind is concerned: males are intellectual on the outside, and affective or loving on the inside; females are affective or loving on the outside and intellectual on the inside.

4.6 Love in 'marriage'

For many couples, love between men and women develops as a couple spend time with each other and get to know and trust each other to a deeper level. However, many of us are unaware of what is taking place spiritually over the course of a growing healthy relationship.

Dr. David Gladish has translated Swedenborg's book *The Sensible Joy in Married Love and The Foolish Pleasures of Illicit Love* to author the book *Love in Marriage*. In this book Swedenborg explains that men and women in loving 'married' relationships have their minds joined in a spiritual union. Here, marriage refers to a committed, nurturing, respectful and supportive union. In the initial stages of union between a man and a women, there is usually some degree of sexual love with heavenly love yet to develop. Later, if heavenly love has developed between the couple, the sexual part of the relationship is derived ever more from heavenly love and the pair are now in what Swedenborg calls married love.

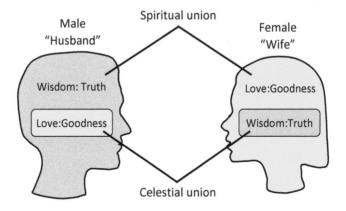

Figure 12 The uniting of heavenly parts of our minds in 'marriage'.

Spiritually, in a relationship between a man and a woman that is for the most part heavenly in nature, the man and woman each become 'joined' in a sense. This happens when they cooperate together during good 'acts', with each other drawing from the other's spirit. The two levels of union are shown in Figure 12. A spiritual union makes use of a man's and woman's external or spiritual level (together they use the spiritual level of their minds). In this case the external will (love or goodness) of the woman operates in union with the man's external understanding or intellect (wisdom or truth). In this situation they will be striving to bring out the heavenly qualities in each other during their interactions as they act with love.

A celestial union between a man and woman is interior in nature (they are using their celestial level of their minds). This type of interaction takes place when the couple are both drawing upon their celestial love of God. As this happens the woman's inner understanding or intellect (wisdom or truth) operates in union with the man's inner will (love or goodness). In this situation the couple will be drawing upon their deep love, feelings, respect and care for each other and all as they follow God's commandments during their interactions.

Swedenborg explains that all beings whether living or not have an aura that surrounds them. As explained earlier, our aura exudes energy in the process of generating our emotions and feelings that belong to our love. Swedenborg was told of the nature of auras by angels who explained that a person's aura wraps around their back and front and is thinner at their back and thicker at their chest. They stated that auric spheres come from every part of our being and extend outward for quite a distance around us. Swedenborg also explains that our auras join or separate a couple outwardly and inwardly. Our auras unite us when we are similar and feel alike. Conversely, our auras make us feel separation from others when there is discord between us. Compatible auric spheres bring about happiness and pleasantness, while discordant spheres bring about unhappiness and unpleasantness. It is through our energetic auric field interactions that we feel the differences and variations of 'married' love.

4.7 Our emotions

Love (experienced as emotion) or on a finer scale affections or goodness (experienced as feelings) are the power behind our ability to create, and human beings have an incredible power and potential to create in all ways and in all areas. The Divine works through our heavenly loves or on a finer scale our heavenly affections or goodness in our will to provide the energy and substance behind what we create. On the other hand, evil spirits work through our hellish loves or on a finer scale evils to provide the energy and substance behind what we destroy (especially our self).

> **Emotions and Feelings:** Pettinelli, *The Psychology of Emotions, Feelings and Thoughts*
>
> Emotion comprises a subconscious and conscious set of feelings that arise during a certain activity or circumstance. Emotion is a component of mood. We have a vague sense of our emotions but a more definite sense of our feelings.

Our intention determines whether we take on-board heavenly influx from the angels around us or hellish influx from the evil spirits around us. The chosen influx then affects some of the heavenly influx from our higher mind that passes through our lower mind. The resulting influx

80

passes into our auric field and then into our body (in particular our brain). This whole process generates our emotions, feelings, thoughts, and actions. If we act with courage and choose heavenly influx, being heavenly love, affections, wisdom, and truths; we will experience positive emotions, feelings, thoughts, and actions and our spiritual and physical wellbeing will be enhanced. In this case we will be growing spiritually. However, if we act from fear and choose hellish influx, being negative or selfish desires and foolishness based on falsity; we will experience negative emotions, feelings, thoughts, and actions and our spiritual and physical wellbeing will deteriorate. This will make us become even more negative, blocked, tired, stale, and ultimately ill, and our spiritual state will be in decay.

Our *positive* emotions include joy, peace, contentment, happiness, gratitude, serenity, hope, confidence, euphoria, and optimism. Our *negative* emotions include anger, guilt, sadness, anxiety, confusion, disgust, annoyance, fear, hatred, apathy, grief, shame, and despair. When we experience negative emotions, our energy centres (chakras) will close to a greater degree and function at a lower level than before. This has the effect of restricting the flow of energy into our auric field's bodies (spiritual, mental, emotional, etheric) and our physical body. As a result, all our bodies become less healthy.

Of most importance to be aware is that when we experience negative emotions, we are corrupting our lower mind, auric field, and physical body. Because of this there is a great need for us to consider the whole situation and keep thoughts positive and realistic. We need to believe in the gifts God has given us and that He works through us to allow us to succeed in our good endeavours. We also need to remind our self that we are all taken care of during our entire existence to eternity. Realising this helps us to relieve ourselves of anxiety or worry. When we live a spiritually healthy life, we can reduce the occurrence and severity of harmful negative emotions. This means living with faith according to God's commandments and spiritual teachings, strengthening our belief system, having compassion, being patient, and accepting and forgiving ourselves and others.

All of us are a work in progress. We will undoubtedly experience negative states of emotions, feelings, thoughts, and actions at various times along our spiritual journey. When we do experience negative emotions, we should not suppress them and cover them over. These times are our opportunities for spiritual growth when we can be more aware of our false beliefs and false values that are justifying our selfish desires that lead to our negative emotions, feelings, thoughts, and actions. We can then seek out truths and make use of our understanding to determine our negative or false beliefs and values. We are then able to dissolve our false beliefs and values through the process of spiritual growth. We do this by taking on true beliefs, values, and practices, and in doing so we grow heavenly loves and affections to displace the hellish loves and evils that are the source of our negative emotions, feelings, thoughts, and actions.

What we do and say is very important, since we can be destructive if we are not careful. Actions including words are the outcome of our intention working with affections (goodness) and cognitions (truths) or desires (evils) and delusions (falsities) in our mind. Because love is behind every emotion, feeling, action, or word we express, it is important to minimise the intensity and frequency when hellish loves (which generate negative emotions) dominate our lives. By doing so we give ourselves the best opportunity to grow spiritually, live well with others, and have good mental and physical health.

4.7.1 Our emotions and healing

All of us at some time or another from early childhood onwards, have been in situations where we have reacted to attacks from others. On many of these occasions we have subjected ourselves to negative emotions and feelings such as guilt, anger, shame, resentment, and despair. Note that no one can make us experience negative emotions. The only way we can experience negative states of being is if we allow ourselves to take onboard negative energy from evil spirits by believing the falsity others are projecting at us. After all, most negative accusations at best are only ever partly true. We are never all bad as is sometimes stated to us. These negative emotions and feelings we take onboard are harmful and destructive to us. Ideally, negative emotions and feelings can be dissipated in a healthy way at the time. Or if we are not ready or able to process them then, they become suppressed by being stored energetically in the second body of our auric field, causing us potential future harm.

Unfortunately for us as children, we are often poorly equipped to process some of our most harmful negative emotions and feelings. We sometimes 'bury' them because dealing with them is very painful, lodging them in our second body of our auric field. Therefore, significant accumulated emotional damage from childhood onwards is often still within us that we are unaware of, being outside our conscious awareness. Even as adults we may be able to recall our experiences logically, yet this does not free us from our past emotional wounds. Often we still have unresolved deep-seated feelings of anger, guilt, shame, resentment, or frustration from the past.

Barbara Brennan explains in her book Light Emerging, that when we suppress these negative emotions and feelings, we cause stagnation in the second body of our auric field. This stagnation then transfers some of the energy-consciousness to our adjacent auric bodies for dissipation (first and third bodies). In our first auric body, the effect of this stagnation is to restrict the energy flow to our physical body. This causes pain, tightness or restriction, and ultimately illness, disease, or sometimes injury if this continues. In our third auric body, the effect is our expression of self-judgment. This self-judgment suppresses our negative emotions even more. If this continues it will cause an emotional depression in us.

When we do deal with our negative emotions in a healthy way, this energy is dissipated and no longer adversely affects us. For us to do this we must first acknowledge the negative emotions we held onto that we were not allowed or ready to show or express, since we can only change what is acknowledged. It is very difficult to change something when we are ignorant of or deny its very existence. Then we need to apply heavenly love by ceasing our self-judgement and proceed to forgive and have patience and compassion for others and our self. We also must proceed to work out our false beliefs that are justifying our negative emotions and feelings. We then choose to live from true beliefs and principles instead. For as we learn to love and have compassion for ourselves in the past, we learn to love and have compassion for ourselves at whatever age we are now, and we become healed.

Some positive & negative mind & body correspondences		
Organ	**Positive correspondence**	**Negative correspondence**
Kidney	Creativity, procreation, and sexuality	Anxiety, fear, and lacking motivation
Liver	Compassion, love, and self-respect	Anger, rage, and primitive emotions
Pancreas	Digestion of ideas and the sweetness of life	Perfectionism and inability to say no

Barbara Brennan also explains that each area of our physical body corresponds to an area of the life of our mind, and so any pain, restriction, illness or injury in that area can be telling us to look at that particular area of our life in our mind. We are emotionally complex, and therefore the reasons for pain in our physical body can be complex. Sometimes, once the emotional cause is discovered and treated, our physical body can recover miraculously fast.

All of us are multi-faceted and interesting on various levels. However, we all hide aspects of ourselves from others for fear we will not be accepted or loved if we show our real self. Although it can be very painful to open up to others at times, it can also allow us to heal and develop to become a more fulfilled and happier person. This allows those around us to see past our selfish aspects to glean aspects of our higher mind, our true self, and love us anyway because they love God's gifts in us.

It's best for us to learn to accept the love of God to come into our life as His Love and Wisdom works through our being and through those around us. Allow the esteem that others have for us to enter our consciousness and become self-esteem. Learn to realise that we have been created as human beings that are perfectly able to take in God's qualities of love and wisdom at any time in our life should we choose to do so. As such, we are always worthy of His love and therefore the love of others.

4.7.2 Kinesiology – an emotional healing modality

We are more able to truly follow our soul's purpose when our mind, auric field, and physical body are aligned. Kinesiology is used to detect the issues in our life to determine what needs to be balanced to promote healing, which can be done in a variety of ways. Kinesiologists typically work with their clients on one of their major emotional issues at a time.

Kinesiology exposed, for the first time, the intimate connection between mind, auric field, and physical body, revealing that when we monitor our muscles, they will test stronger for true propositions and weaker for false propositions. For many people, the results of kinesiological muscle monitoring have been found to be predictable, repeatable, and universal. As such, clinical kinesiological muscle monitoring has found widespread verification and growing usage since the 1990's.

Kinesiologists use kinesiological muscle monitoring in conjunction with charts and their own thought processes to determine the emotional issues of their clients. Once the issue(s) are found, they use muscle monitoring to determine the remedies to assist their clients to heal on all levels. These remedies include the application of essences, oils, to working on chakras using crystals and vibrating instruments, having their clients repeat affirmations, using special purpose music and sounds, and applying energy healing.

Charles Krebb and Tania O'Neill McGowan explain in their book *Energy Kinesiology,* that kinesiology provides access to our holographic or whole humanity; our mind, our auric field, and our physical being – in essence, all the realms of our being that can impact our health. As such, kinesiology is a truly remarkable healing therapy.

5 Spiritual Development

Spiritual development takes place with all of us throughout our lives as we freely choose our own responses to situations, to others, and life generally. At the end of our life, our dominant or ruling love will be either heavenly or hellish. Swedenborg teaches that <u>all</u> people are born capable of becoming angels. Any one of us, whether religious or non-religious, can become an angel if we do our best to live in loving harmony with other people in accordance with what we genuinely believe to be true, and we tend to avoid evil actions. It is the makeup of our spirit in terms of our ruling love that is vitally important, and not so much whether we believe in God or not. If we pass over to an angelic community, we will be given instruction to understand the true reality of God.

In every moment of our lives we have choices between thoughts and actions that are directed to the greater good of all or to serve our selfish purposes. As part of our total mind processes, the spiritual influences filter into our conscious awareness and present themselves to our choice processes. We need to develop spiritually so we can become aware of these spiritual influences, especially the cunning and persuasive hellish ones. This awareness helps us to decide to reject hellish influences and instead take on-board good influences so we can achieve consistent spiritual growth by allowing God to work through us. Provided our decisions and actions are motivated by heavenly love, they will affect and transform the inner recesses of our mind and we will have greater periods of peace, joy, and happiness. Our spiritual growth takes place whenever we resist selfish desires that are directed solely toward our own benefit and instead act for the greatest good of all.

If through our life we are to have God push our selfish-loves aside and develop our love for Him, others, and all of creation, then we must live a life based on use and service. Through friendship, service to others, and receiving help from others, we gain a greater appreciation of the gift of life and acknowledgement of God. This pattern of new life is a universal process that applies to all cultures in which all people who consistently apply spiritual truths in their life through goodness are prepared for heaven.

We are in a state of spiritual health when our mind is in the love of what is good and true; those things which bring us lasting delight and positive thoughts we love to dwell on. Spiritual health automatically involves our own personal growth and a genuine concern for the welfare of others. This in turn brings inner peace, humility, joy, faith, and spiritual riches beyond measure. If we are caught up in fear, worry, hatred, anger, greed, lust for power, revenge, and so on, we are in a state of spiritual ill health.

5.1 Our proprium and heavenly proprium

Many of us think that each of us exists as a being who is separate from all other life. The reality is that all of us are connected to everyone else and all of creation by the flow of life from God into us and to all of creation. Swedenborg uses the term proprium for the false sense or awareness that we are a separate, self-contained person, with a mind and physical body of our own quite apart from God, other persons, and all created things. Proprium is what lies behind our 'I-ness' or self-identity. It is our proprium's interpretation of what it sees and feels with our physical body's senses that creates the great illusion into which we fall – the belief that we are separate and independent from everyone and everything in this world and the rest of the universe. Since this appearance, despite being so strong, is an illusion, our proprium itself can be said to not *really* exist. It only seems like we have a proprium. Since God lives from Himself, only He has an actual or living Proprium which is Life itself. We can only have what appears to us as a proprium because we are alive from His Proprium.

When we see life from our proprium, we tend to see life relative to our self. In this case our desires or needs and actions are seen in isolation from those of others and all things. We are living from both our own and inherited evils and not from God. During these times when we live from our proprium, we draw upon evil and falsity from evil spirits and therefore we are in some degree of delusion. Our evil desires appear to us as good and are justified by falsity which we deem to be truth, and good appears as evil. In this state our motivating love is hellish.

As we grow spiritually, God gradually pushes our proprium aside, and over time creates in our mind a heavenly proprium in our will and understanding in our lower mind, which differs from our proprium. Now our conscience is developing. He gives us affection for good and for seeking and living truth from that good. Instead of living from a self-centred focus, our perception, values, and expectations shift towards doing good for others and our self in our life. Our love and understanding have changed to become more heavenly.

If we are growing spiritually, we will have an ever-growing heavenly proprium and conscience. We will also have more peace and tranquillity, faith, happiness, and joy, since our higher mind and heavenly aspects of our lower mind are exerting a greater influence in our life. This relieves us of some of our self-love, conflict, hatred, anger, resentment, anxiety, greed, revenge, and fear. We can rest assured that our life is in God's hands. This heavenly proprium which we receive, is filled by God in the next life with delights and happiness beyond comprehension. For God desires to give to all of us what is His - that is what is heavenly, so that it may appear as our own for us to live by, although it is not ours.

Our proprium is never to be annihilated, as it is necessary for us to function in the world as an individual. When we make heavenly choices, we cease living from our proprium. This is as true of the angelic state after death as it is in this life, for without a proprium there is no freedom of choice. The angels are left perpetually free to receive love and wisdom rather than live from their proprium. When angels are in their proprium they are sad and hope to soon return to their former state into heaven again. For them it is heaven when they withhold themselves from their proprium.

5.2 Our conscience

We all have a complex and multifaceted set of loves from God in our higher mind and in our will in our lower mind, where each love is comprised of a set of affections or goodness. Our conscience comes about from affections in our will in our lower mind working with truths in our lower mind's understanding to generate feelings, perceptions, and thoughts that guide us or warn us in situations so the greatest good can result. Conscience guides us towards goodness, a spiritual quality and quantity, and is not driven by our rational mind since this only provides an estimate of fairness or equity, not goodness. Following our conscience is following God; otherwise we are being selfish.

Conscience arises by the activity of angels connected and associated with us, awakening what Swedenborg refers to as our remains - our heavenly affections or goodness and their associated truths, good feelings, and memories. The angels call forth the forms of goodness and truth residing with us and set them opposite the evils and falsities influencing our mind that are activated by evil spirits connected and associated with us.

Swedenborg explains that we have three levels of heavenly love in our will: celestial, spiritual, and spiritual-natural. This means that depending on the situation, we may be drawing God's influx mainly through one of our spiritual loves to guide us at a particular moment in our life. Alternatively, in another situation or moment, we may draw God's influx mainly through one of our celestial loves, provided we have that higher love in our being for Him to act through. The more we develop the higher levels of our conscience, the greater good, peace, joy, and happiness we can experience in our life.

Our conscience grows stronger and truer as we grow spiritually, and we do this by seeking high quality truths and applying them through goodness in our life. As we do so, we resist our selfish inclinations experienced during temptations. Sacred scriptures such as the Bible will show us many truths if we search for them, with every story driving home some point about truth. We should always be working to develop our conscience to make it truer and stronger.

Whenever we go against our conscience by choosing selfish practices, we take into our lower mind the evil desires and falsities of the evil spirits tempting us. This has the effect of restricting and distorting some of the influx from our higher mind that passes through our lower mind, turning it into evil and falsity, and corrupting our lower mind, auric field, and physical body. Then later, when through fear justified by our delusions, we draw upon their evils in our lower mind and allow the evil spirits to control us. This further reinforces the strength of these evils and our false beliefs or delusions. By restricting and distorting some of the influx from our higher mind and corrupting our lower mind, we have eroded and degraded our conscience, lowered our level of consciousness, and weakened our ability to live a heavenly life.

Humility

Remembering that all the power we have in our conscience comes from God, belongs to God, and is ours to use, will help to prevent us becoming proud of what we are doing and thinking that we are superior to others.

We can either act from conscience when we are good to others and our self or be troubled by conscience when we are being selfish. When we choose to be selfish and ignore our conscience, we will initially suffer some degree of inner anguish and torment. When we do this, we restrict and distort some of the influx from our higher mind, our lower mind is corrupted, and our conscience is eroded. If we choose to continue in this way, we will ultimately experience a deathly apathy, which is the sign that our conscience has greatly diminished and is therefore less able to serve us well.

Swedenborg explains that in situations where we have heavenly goods and truths to live by in our being, God is constantly dissipating evils and falsities by inner means through our conscience. However, when we encounter situations where we have not developed heavenly goods and truths to live by, hence we do not have a conscience for those situations; our lives are regulated externally through a fear of the law and fear of loss of life, honour, wealth, and consequent reputation. It is these restraints that maintain some degree of order and civility in our world. Note that when we experience fear of being caught doing wrong and disgrace it may seem like our conscience is active, however, this is not so and is simply an appearance.

5.3 Spiritual growth

As stated previously, we inherit hellish loves and evil ways (hereditary evils) from our ancestors. New hellish loves will be added to our lower mind and our existing hellish loves in our lower mind will strengthen unless we resist selfish desires by following God. Jesus said that we must be born again "of the Spirit" with a new outlook on our life. We do this by turning away from being self-centred and instead live our life by what we understand to be true from a spiritual sense. This allows God's direct influx and indirect influx from angels around us to gift our higher mind and lower mind respectively with heavenly qualities, being love and wisdom, goodness and truth.

Our new self is conceived from God's gifts in us and takes place over the course of the rest of our life. Note that it is not possible for this process to take place in a short period. This is because we need time and opportunities to recognise each selfish aspect of us that needs changing, learn and understand or rationalise new truths, and then work to overcome those aspects for the desired changes to take place. As we develop spiritually, we experience greater periods of joy, happiness, peace, faith, contentment, improved mental and physical health, stronger and deeper friendships, and more loving relationships with others.

Gaining spiritual qualities:

As part of God's gifts of love and wisdom given during our spiritual growth, we can develop/enhance the following qualities and more:

altruism	caring	clarity of mind
commitment	compassion	dependability
emotional stability	encouragement	endurance
faith	fearlessness	forgiveness
generosity	genuineness	goodness
happiness	helpfulness	honesty
humility	innocence	kindness
mindfulness	modesty	optimism
patience	peace	perceptiveness
playfulness	reliability	see good in others
selflessness	sensibility	sincerity
unconditional love	usefulness	warmth

As Swedenborg explains, the benefits from spiritual growth in this life flow on to the next life when we live in a heavenly community where love to God and mutual love between all are a constant way of life. Angels in heaven live a life of use to God and to others, including us. Everyone there is supremely happy, employed in a way for which they are uniquely fit. They carry out the work they love for the greatest benefit of all in their communities. For them it is a great delight to be of utmost use and benefit to their society and to us.

Whenever we choose evil ways, we act on selfish motives, reject and turn away from God, and separate ourselves from others and life generally. During these periods, evil spirits subsequently punish us with their attacks, inducing selfish desires and false thoughts and stir up memories so we suffer from states including anger, guilt, shame, anxiety, and fear. However, when we choose heavenly ways, our lower mind is aligned with our higher mind and we cease to suffer these conflicts. We are then in conjunction with God and in a peaceful state of tranquillity, experiencing positive emotions such as happiness, joy, contentment, and optimism. As we succeed to shun evil ways, God suppresses evermore the influence of our proprium and our selfish desires shrivel and lose power in us. He then grows our will and understanding that contains His goodness and truth, in the process developing our heavenly proprium and conscience. This gives us more of His heavenly gifts which we draw upon as we live less and less from our old selfish desires, lusts, greed, and false beliefs.

Note that spiritual growth is a cyclic recurrence throughout our life, with each cycle lasting varying lengths of time dependent on the severity and nature of the hellish love and false understanding or delusion being worked on at the time. Importantly, to grow spiritually requires us to work with God – we cannot do this on our own. All we can do is say no to our egotistic and selfish desires. God does the actual battling with evil spirits during temptation while we battle with intent only. Then as our heavenly will grows in us, we continue to follow its loving urges. We open our self more to God and His Life floods into us more fully. We then become a more loving and wise person.

It is the state of our ruling love, being heavenly or hellish, at the end of our life that determines the spiritual community we will live in after our death. Most importantly, the development of our ruling love takes place only during our physical lifetime. Swedenborg states that after a person dies and passes into the spiritual world, becoming a spirit, their ruling love will not change. Beware that however high we may rise during our life in the physical world, we may end up misusing our freewill and drop 'down', ending up in a hellish community.

5.3.1 Spiritual growth process

Gaining an understanding of the spiritual growth process allows us to more effectively apply our spiritual learnings along our life's journey for maximum benefit. Swedenborg refers to each cycle of the spiritual growth process as a series of three stages: repentance, reformation, and regeneration as shown in Figure 13 ahead.

Repentance, reformation, and regeneration are all about movement onwards from a fear-based guilt-ridden state, to a more loving state based on forgiveness, salvation, and new directions. As explained previously, we have remains or remnant states of heavenly experiences within our being that are our seeds of growth. These have been implanted in our lower mind from conception onwards. To allow us to progress to less selfish and eventually loving states, angels with us gently stir our remains to lead us to good.

Originally, many of us are dominated by a selfish motivation toward life, so a new heavenly will needs to be allowed to grow for us to draw upon as our old selfish desires shrivel.

We must 'own' our wrong doings; recognise them, take responsibility for them, and accept them for repentance, reformation, and regeneration to proceed. During repentance, reformation, and regeneration, God gives and unites goodness and truth in both our higher mind and lower mind so that our love to act from this goodness and truth strengthens, and we experience more happiness, joy, peace, and contentment.

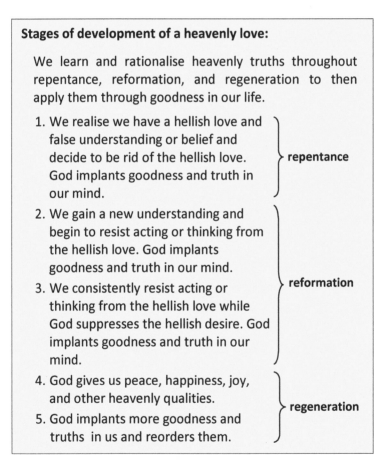

Stages of development of a heavenly love:

We learn and rationalise heavenly truths throughout repentance, reformation, and regeneration to then apply them through goodness in our life.

1. We realise we have a hellish love and false understanding or belief and decide to be rid of the hellish love. God implants goodness and truth in our mind. } **repentance**

2. We gain a new understanding and begin to resist acting or thinking from the hellish love. God implants goodness and truth in our mind.

3. We consistently resist acting or thinking from the hellish love while God suppresses the hellish desire. God implants goodness and truth in our mind. } **reformation**

4. God gives us peace, happiness, joy, and other heavenly qualities.

5. God implants more goodness and truths in us and reorders them. } **regeneration**

Figure 13 Our spiritual growth process.

Swedenborg explains in his book *New Jerusalem and its Heavenly Doctrine,* that the knowledge we gain relating to our physical and spiritual life stored in our memory, opens the way to our spiritual development. This memory knowledge, especially memory knowledge of spiritual truth, are the receptacles and vessels for the truth and goodness taken in by our mind . Note that the truths are distributed in groupings and united according to the love and affections which introduced them. They are our means to which we gain love and wisdom.

Repentance

Many people today think only of a mind being made 'smarter,' but not of its whole nature being changed. The first thing we need to do to achieve a change in nature to one of a more heavenly disposition is to repent by examining the way we live. We need to see some of the more obvious ways that we are selfish, how our selfishness is destructive and separates us from God, others, and life generally, and then accept that we must change and align with God.

Repentance takes place in stages over time and means to undergo a change in frame of mind and feeling – to think differently, taking on a new attitude for goodness. It involves examining our self to recognise and acknowledge our selfish ways, to take responsibility for them, to admit them to God, to ask for help and power to overcome them, and by doing so to lead a new life, and to do all these things as from our self.

Evils cannot eventually be pushed aside unless they appear to us. Therefore, we must examine the quality of our motivations or what it is we love and desire along with our thoughts and actions, especially considering what we would do if we were not afraid of punishment by the law or of being disgraced. Our understanding, which is separate from our will, allows this examination to take place. We are able to see that we have selfish motivations and that we should resist our selfish acts. We should work to acknowledge evils in our lower mind (repentance) so that we make possible our progress through to the subsequent stages of reformation and regeneration.

Reformation

After our change in attitude and recognising evils, comes reformation, where we turn away from our evils and refrain from acting from them. As Swedenborg explains, to resist one evil is to resist many; for every evil is connected with countless other evils. During the process of reformation, evil spirits with us stir up the evils within us to tempt us with evil desires. Most of our evil or hellish tendencies are well disguised and hidden deep down below our conscious awareness. At the same time, God via the angels with us stirs up our goodness and truth (our remains implanted throughout our life) while acting through our conscience to show us what is right and lead us towards good. The resulting spiritual process, called temptation, is between the evil spirits with us and God with us. Temptations serve to soften our vessels that receive genuine truth so that they are then in a state to receive genuine goodness. Note that the 'goodness' and 'truth' we have taken into our being as we learn 'truth' in our life are appearances of genuine truth and genuine goodness. Only God has actual or genuine goodness and truth. During reformation we are introduced to genuine goodness and genuine truth that displaces our appearances of truth and goodness. When the process of reformation is complete, we intuitively make use of genuine goodness and genuine truth instead of non-genuine goodness and non-genuine truth and the non-genuine truth fades from our memory.

> **Our three types of temptation:** Lazer, *Temptations*
>
> 1. *Celestial temptations* (most grievous) – against our love to God.
> 2. *Spiritual temptations* – against our charity or love towards others.
> 3. *Natural temptations* – not actual temptations but anxious cares resulting from attacks on our natural loves caused by misfortune and sickness.
>
> Before we undergo temptations, God arranges our goodness and truths to prepare us to resist the evils and falsities which are with us (stirred up by evil spirits).

During temptations we feel doubts, evil promptings, and we suffer from confusion and distress. Temptations are carried to their ultimate state (which for grievous temptations is generally desperation), so that we can receive maximum benefit when we overcome them. The degree of temptation is in proportion to the depth of heavenly love and wisdom, goodness and truth that we have in our being and is being attacked. Celestial temptations are against our love to God and are most grievous when they are accompanied with bodily pains; and still more so when those pains endure and no deliverance is granted, even though the person begs for Divine mercy.

Swedenborg explains that prayers to overcome temptation are not heeded during temptation. This is because any act to end the temptation would defeat its very purpose of subduing selfishness in us so that goodness and truth can be implanted in our higher mind and in our lower mind's will and understanding. Victory over the evil is achieved through our willingness to acknowledge that it is God's power fighting for us while we feel as though all the effort was our own. In this way, we are united with God and allow Him to work through us.

Swedenborg explains that during temptations we have an interior motive of love for God and His kingdom. When we engage in the spiritual battle of temptation, we resolve our self to subdue the evil with sufficient strength to equal the force and determination of the evil assaulting us. The freedom we have during this struggle is from God via the angels with us and leads us to feel as if we are conquering the evil under our own power. Without us feeling as though we have won the spiritual battle on our own through freedom, we cannot be reformed, since love and wisdom, and on a finer scale goodness and truth, can only be given in freedom.

Success during reformation occurs as we are able to consistently sustain our struggle against our selfishness up to and including the final and most severe temptation battle. Following a successful period of reformation, angels then drive the evil spirits (who were harassing and tempting us) well outside our region of influence. This makes room for the reception of goodness and truth in our higher mind and in the heavenly part of our lower mind. Now we will have angels close by influencing us to give us support. While our state during temptation was of struggle, confusion, and distress; after temptation God leaves us in a much more peaceful, clear, and settled state, and we feel consoled. By the end of the process of reformation, our recollection of the non-genuine truths in our memory fades, these being replaced by genuine truths in our understanding that we know intuitively. Hence, we gain perception and wisdom and a corresponding higher level of consciousness.

Regeneration

Eventually following the victorious final temptation battle, God gives us more goodness and truth directly into our higher mind. He also gives us more goodness and truth indirectly into our lower mind via the angels now with us, who experience happiness and joy and so do we. God reorders our goodness and truth and arranges it in a heavenly form. He opens our interior sight (understanding) giving us greater wisdom, intelligence, and enlightenment. Now we have a deeper intuitive knowing of truths, being greater faith. Also, both our higher mind and lower mind become associated with a higher society in heaven and we receive inner peace and humility. This has the effect of further raising our level of consciousness in this world and lifts us into more heavenly states of love and affection and greater awareness and perception.

Being associated with a higher spiritual society in heaven creates a stronger link between heaven and the world in us. This gives God with us the ability to provide greater heavenly influence or influx and order into our consciousness. He is then able to implant more truths and forms of goodness into our higher mind and lower mind and strengthen those already there. Both the quality and strength of our heavenly proprium and conscience will grow and we will have a more heavenly nature. We are now able to act more consistently and from a deeper level of heavenly love than before. We also receive greater enlightenment and perception as to what is good and true and evil and false, giving us greater faith, intelligence, and wisdom as a result of truths. As a result we gain a higher level of consciousness.

After success through temptation, our higher mind acquires greater dominion over our lower mind, further subduing our hellish love of self and love of the world and making us humbler. We become more receptive to the life of heaven from God, which is the life of a re-born person. We gain goodness and truth which dominates our evil (our love of self and love of the world). However, yielding in temptations goes against God as evils and falsities are confirmed against goodness and truth in our lower mind. This leads to a greater restriction of influx from our higher mind into our lower mind, our lower mind becomes further corrupted, and our auric field and physical body suffers. We then end up experiencing a greater quantity and level of negative emotions, feelings, and thoughts and we suffer a substantial lowering of our level of consciousness.

Eventually, after a successful temptation battle, we feel delight as we express heavenly love in our life and a new part of our 're-born self' is formed. Then our spiritual development continues when another part of our selfishness must be seen and conquered, and we face another and different battle with temptation. Battles can be brief, in a sudden moment, or drawn out over a long period of life as we struggle against our evils. The duration of our battles depends on the kind and intensity of selfishness in us that we must conquer. During our continuing process of spiritual growth, we tend to be confronted with one evil above others for us to work against and overcome - in line with what we can handle. Once that evil is overcome (pushed outside our sphere of influence), another evil will come into our awareness. God knows what we can cope with. He prepares us, protects us, and fights for us as evil spirits mount their spiritual attacks against the heavenly gifts in our being.

Success through temptation by living according to the spiritual lessons we have learned not only opens the rational degree of our lower mind but also transforms it, gradually changing its quality from natural to more spiritual. What is 'above' in our higher mind – that is, charity or love to others (the spiritual level) and love for God (the celestial) – gradually flow down into our rational degree, enhancing its quality. The rational degree of our mind is gradually transformed and developed from 'above' by our higher mind and becomes less natural in quality and more spiritual or celestial, depending on which of these qualities is flowing in from our higher mind.

A similar process takes place with the middle degree of our lower mind. It is gradually developed from 'above' as the heavenly qualities of our transformed rational degree gradually flow down into it. The middle degree is then transformed and also becomes more spiritual or celestial in quality. Then finally, the sensual degree of our lower mind gradually becomes subject to the transformed middle degree above it and is put in alignment with heaven as far as possible. Then we are transformed more so on all levels and degrees of our mind. This process of development is discussed and shown previously in Figure 8 on page 56.

From conception, we experience natural growth from the lowest degree of our lower mind to the highest degree of our lower mind. However, during spiritual growth, there is a descent from our higher mind down to the lowest degree of our lower mind as shown in Figure 14. As this takes place, influx from our lower mind flows into our auric field and enhances our fourth auric body and our three higher auric bodies. Our three higher auric bodies in-turn enhance and harmonise our three lowest auric bodies. This has the effect of giving us a higher proportion of positive emotions, feelings, thoughts, ideas, actions, and expression of our true self in our daily life. We also experience improved physical health and healthier relationships with others and all of life in general.

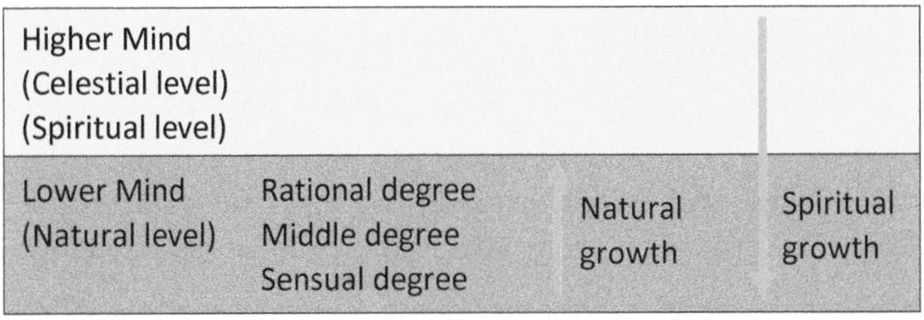

Higher Mind (Celestial level) (Spiritual level)			
Lower Mind (Natural level)	Rational degree Middle degree Sensual degree	Natural growth	Spiritual growth

Figure 14 Ascent pre-re-birth and descent during spiritual growth
(adapted from Rev. D. Taylor's The Hidden Levels of the Mind).

Swedenborg explains that no hereditary evils or those we take into our lower mind during our time in the physical world are ever separated from us. During spiritual growth, the evils we have overcome are pushed aside and hidden from us, so they do not exert a direct influence over us. They are thrust from our centre of influence to the periphery and we then experience peace from them. As such, we can at any time deliberately return to these evils if we choose to do so. If we do, we restrict the flow of influx from our higher mind, corrupt our lower mind with more evil and falsity, erode its goodness and truth, and degrade our conscience.

This is dire and is known as profanation or sinning against the Holy Spirit (Mark 3:28-30). In this case we coldly rationalise and confirm an evil when we clearly know better. Sinning against the Holy Spirit cannot be wiped away or 'forgiven' because we have deliberately through freewill confirmed evil and falsity. God accepts our spiritual choices and always has infinite love for us. If in the future we wish to be alleviated from this evil, we must work through the process of repentance, reformation, and regeneration.

The implanting of truth into our lower mind takes place whenever we use the rational part of our mind to develop an understanding and belief of non-genuine truth and then go on to develop a love of genuine truth (faith) in our lower mind. Sinning against the Son of Man (Mark 3:28-30) takes place when we go against the non-genuine truth in our memory only that has not yet led to the implanting of genuine truth into our lower mind. In this case we don't have associated genuine truth in our lower mind and so it can't be corrupted. Therefore this act can be 'forgiven'.

6 Consciousness

The word 'consciousness' is used and defined in various ways in the writings of many spiritual traditions. In essence, Consciousness is Life from God, being His Love and Wisdom proceeding as an infinite field of energy (creative potential and creation). Reality is all of life being animate or not that has ever existed, and is recorded in this field of life energy that we call Consciousness. Importantly, there is but one Consciousness and all of life is connected to this Consciousness.

Our consciousness results from the overall degree in which life energy, being Love and Wisdom from the Divine, works through us in our life. This life or energy from the Divine passing through our being gives us an awareness in various states or finite perception of the overall Reality. In Swedenborg's terms we have perception or a level of faith that allows us to perceive aspects of God's Life or Reality, giving us wisdom and true intelligence. As our spiritual state changes from moment-to-moment through our life, so does our perception of Reality. It is the combined effect of our spiritual choices throughout our life that ultimately determines our consciousness in our being and our ability to see aspects of the overall Reality.

As we develop spiritually, we exercise greater spiritual power in our life and gain greater awareness of the overall reality of life. This means that the way we see the world changes for the better to be truer. We see life more for what it truly is – the good and the bad. We experience a shift in seeing the world from a less fearful and harmful perspective, to a truer one where there is more hope and a greater awareness of goodness in people and events.

Gaining an appreciation of what consciousness is in terms of our varying stages of spiritual development gives us a reference to see our progression spiritually on our journey and 'where' we might end up.

6.1 States and levels of consciousness

Now we take a closer look at what is meant by states and levels of consciousness. Levels of consciousness represent the spiritual power from the Divine that flows through our being, which directly indicates our actual milestones of spiritual growth. We are complex beings and as we grow, we develop many different aspects (being loves and associated wisdoms) to our spiritual makeup. Life energy from the Divine flows through each aspect according to the degree of its spiritual development. As such, each aspect of our being has its own unique level of consciousness. Our overall level of consciousness is the combined effect of these various aspects. Life from the Divine flowing through our mind gives us a perception of aspects of Consciousness. As such, amazingly, our mind is a finite transceiver of Consciousness, giving us some awareness of the greater Reality.

Ken Wilber describes in his book *Integral Spirituality*, the major states of consciousness of our mind as waking, dreaming, and deep sleep. We can also experience other states such as those stimulated by listening to exquisite music, experiencing nature, meditative states, drug-induced states, etc. All states of consciousness are temporary, coming and going over relatively short time periods. Importantly, Wilber also explains that while our states of consciousness readily change, our levels of consciousness are semi-permanent and don't usually change much over long periods of time. Interestingly, Wilber explains that

110

meditation can temporarily shift us to higher states of consciousness but will not shift us to higher levels of consciousness, just 'lubricate' the path. This means that when we meditate we can move to higher states of consciousness while in these meditative states, however, when we cease meditating we will 'come down' from those states to our 'resting' level of consciousness.

We as individuals are an integral part of infinite Consciousness. How we identify with ourselves and life depends on our level and state of consciousness. Whether we're happy or sad, fearful or loving, healthy or ill, our experience derives from our level and state of consciousness. During our life our state and level of consciousness will increase or decrease as a result of our spiritual choices. As we grow spiritually, God's influx works through our being to a greater extent and the levels of our mind and auric field operate at higher vibrational frequencies and with greater coherency. This gives us a higher level of consciousness along with the ability to experience higher states of consciousness or higher levels of perception. We will then have more of our true self being expressed in our personality and experience greater heavenly impact in our life.

> *It's only when our state or level of consciousness changes that our experience of reality changes.*

Sir David R. Hawkins, M.D., Ph.D., is an internationally renowned psychiatrist, consciousness researcher, spiritual lecturer, and mystic. In his book *Power vs. Force*, Dr. Hawkins explains that everything in the universe is connected with everything else to create a 'database' of consciousness that is available from the present time and going back in time. Once we learn how to, our mind allows us to tap into information stored in consciousness in a powerful way that is not possible using artificial intelligence.

Table 2 Consciousness levels (Power vs. Force, Dr. D. Hawkins).

Consciousness Level	Emotion	Energy (Log base 10 in points)
Enlightenment	Ineffable	700-1000
Peace	Bliss	600
Joy	Serenity	540
Love	Reverence	500
Reason	Understanding	400
Acceptance	Forgiveness	350
Willingness	Optimism	310
Neutrality	Trust	250
Courage ———	Affirmation ———	200 ———
Pride	Scorn	175
Anger	Hate	150
Desire	Craving	125
Fear	Anxiety	100
Grief	Regret	75
Apathy	Despair	50
Guilt	Blame	30
Shame	Humiliation	20

Power (Truth) / Force (Falsity)

Dr. Hawkins and his team have researched and categorised the various states and levels of consciousness and associated emotional states and levels of enlightenment that people have reached throughout history. In doing so they have developed a profile of the human condition and what has become a popular model of the various levels of consciousness and their associated emotions (see Table 2). To do this they performed millions of kinesiological muscle monitoring tests on thousands of subjects around the world, varying in age, personality, and background, over a twenty-year period. The tests have proved to be reproduceable in scientific terms.

The basis of kinesiological muscle monitoring tests works as follows for many people. Note that for test results to be reliable, the person doing the testing and the person under test both need to have a level of consciousness above what is defined as courage in Table 2. When we are in a selfish state (falsity) such as shame, guilt, confusion, fear, hatred, pride, and hopelessness; non-true or negative life energy fields pass from our lower mind through our auric field and into our physical body. These energy fields generate negative emotions, feelings, thoughts, and induce a weaker muscle response. In contrast, when we are in a heavenly state (truth) such as courage, acceptance, reason, compassion, joy, and peace; positive life energy fields pass from our lower mind through our auric field and into our body. These energy fields generate positive emotions, feelings, thoughts, and uplift life. In these states of being our muscle response stays stronger. Dr. Hawkins and his team have used muscle monitoring to evaluate the truth of various statements covering a wide array of topics to research and categorise their work.

The life energy that flows through us at the various consciousness levels varies enormously from the lower levels of consciousness to the upper levels. Because the values in numerical terms vary so greatly, the energy levels in Table 2 are represented logarithmically as 'points'. What this means is that a consciousness energy of 200 points is not twice that of 100 points. For a one point increase in consciousness energy in the table, the actual consciousness energy value increases tenfold. An increase in consciousness level means that we are becoming more loving and wise. Conversely, a decrease in consciousness level means we are becoming more selfish and foolish. Therefore, if our consciousness energy as per the table was to increase by 1 point from 150 points to 151 points, we would have increased our actual consciousness energy value by a factor of ten. Likewise, if we were to shift our consciousness energy as per the table by 2 points from 150 points to 152 points, we would increase our actual consciousness energy value by a factor of one hundred (ten raised to the power of 2). So, an increase of even a few points of consciousness energy represents a major advance in spiritual power.

Note that Table 2 shows a split in the levels of consciousness. All levels with energy below 200 points represent spiritual states of force (selfishness and falsity) that are destructive of life on all levels: for the person, their society, and the larger world. In contrast, all levels with energy above 200 points represent power (love to all and truth) and enhance life. The level of courage (200 energy points) is importantly the balance point that separates the levels of force (or falsity) from the levels of power (or truth). As such, when our consciousness energy is below 200 points, we are predominantly in selfish and fear-based states and are an overall drain on society. When our consciousness energy is above 200 points, we are predominantly in states of goodness (true courage) and are an overall benefit to society.

Importantly, it is possible given success in the most grievous of temptation battles, for us to ultimately increase our consciousness energy by 100 points or more during spiritual growth. This represents an enormous increase in energy value (ten to the power of 100 or more). Therefore, the rate of increase in power as we grow spiritually and move up the scale can be enormous. This means that people who are spiritually well developed exert a vastly greater positive influence on the world than those at lower levels and counteract those below consciousness level courage (200 energy points). Note that much of their beneficial influence is taking place outside their conscious awareness. Likewise, when we are in selfish states most of our destructive influence is taking place outside our conscious awareness.

As we grow spiritually, we progressively rise in the level of our consciousness and the 'frequency' or 'vibration' of energy of our mind and auric field increases. When we are at a high enough level (and state) of consciousness (above courage), we radiate a beneficial and healing effect on the world. As our consciousness evolves to reaching more positive levels, we naturally strive to seek means and ways to further this advancement as our heavenly life develops. Throughout history, all the world's great religions and spiritual disciplines have striven to learn and employ practices that allow people to ascend through the levels of consciousness.

6.2 Several consciousness levels explained

The book *Power vs. Force* by Dr. Hawkins explains the various levels of consciousness. Shown ahead are explanations of some of the levels of consciousness we can experience. We can use this 'map' of the levels of consciousness as a reference to see where we sit on the 'map.' By gaining an appreciation of what these levels of consciousness are like, we can also gauge how we might advance to higher levels in the future.

Energy level 100 points is Fear, which is the driver behind a great deal of activity for much of the world's population. Some of the more common fears include fear of death, fear of loss of relationship, fear of those who hold hatred towards us, fear of loss of employment, fear of being disliked or unloved, etc. These fears and more can be major motivators for many of us. When we are living at this level of consciousness, we allow our fears to have a large influence in our life. Through our level of consciousness we perceive reality, and so many of the events around us become perceived as fearful. This can lead us to become paranoid or neurotic which creates a great deal of stress. In turn, we can induce fear into others which can lead to wider spread social fears. Of most importance is that being in fearful states inhibits our personal (spiritual) growth.

Energy level 200 points is Courage, where at this critical energy level we are willing to face the difficult situations in our life and try new ways of overcoming them. We are able to confront our fears, anxieties, and personal deficiencies. In doing so we are able to grow through these experiences that often would be too much for those of us at lower levels of consciousness. At this level of consciousness we are in a balance where we are putting as much life energy into the world as we are taking. The net effect of people at levels lower than this is that on average they drain life energy from society.

Energy level 250 points is Neutrality, where a person has the ability to rise above challenges that dissipate their energies to allow flexibility, a nonjudgmental outlook, and a realistic appraisal of problems. At this level of consciousness we are relatively unattached to outcomes. We don't feel that we have to get our way with things; and when we don't, we can accept that position. We are gaining a sense of inner confidence and power. This makes us less likely to be intimidated and no longer having a strong need to prove our position. We are not so interested in conflict, competition, or being right all the time. Because of this, when we are at this level of consciousness we are relatively easy to get along with and typically safe to associate with.

Energy level 350 points is Acceptance, where a major transformation takes place, with the appreciation that we are the source and creator of our life's experiences. At this level of consciousness our respect and belief in equality is established and we see others as having the same rights as us. We are no longer drawn to conflict or opposition. We have become much less rigid in our views and are now much more accepting of the wishes of our broader society when it comes to finding ways to address society's issues. We are now much more tolerant of others and less likely to discriminate within our society.

Energy level 400 points is Reason, where we are able to make rapid and correct decisions, manipulate symbols, and understand relationships between things. Reason is highly effective in the technical world that is dominated by methodologies based on logic. However, reason is limited in the ability to discern what truly underlies a complex issue and generally disregards context. It does not in itself provide a guide to truth. Importantly, reason often becomes the major block to reaching higher levels of consciousness. Only 8 percent of the world's population operates at the consciousness energy levels in the 400's of points and it is relatively uncommon for people to transcend this level.

Energy level 500 points is Love, which is unconditional and has ongoing momentum that doesn't shift easily or often. When we are at this level of consciousness, the dominant source of love within us is heavenly and does not depend on external self-centred conditions. Our loving is a state of being derived from our inner state, not external conditions. Love is not intellectual and so does not proceed from our rational mind. Love emanates from our inner goodness and is expressed as positive emotions. When we are at this level of consciousness, we relate to the world in a forgiving, nurturing, supportive, compassionate, and patient way, and we have a capacity to lift others and accomplish great feats.

At this level we are able to instantaneously understand without resorting to analytical thinking using our rational mind. This ability is known as intuition. [Swedenborg explains in his book *New Jerusalem and its Heavenly Doctrine* that as a person grows spiritually, they become more loving, wise, intelligent, and experience greater perception of what is good and true without needing to rationalise]. Love looks to the goodness in life, seeing the positives that are always present. It looks at what some may see as negative situations and sees that there is also goodness inherent in all of life. We experience true happiness when we are at this level of consciousness which is reached by only 4 percent of the world's population.

Energy level 540 points is Joy, where unconditional love is experienced as an inner Joy. At this level of consciousness we are not experiencing fleeting periods of joy from external events. Instead, we are feeling an ongoing and deep-seated joy derived from within that underpins all our activities, independent of external events. We are experiencing joy within most of our moments of life - this joy is not the pleasure we get from self-centred pursuits.

At this level of consciousness we are very compassionate and may sometimes gaze in an open and caring manner at others for extended periods, inducing a state of love and peace. At this energy level we have great capacity for patience and the ability to persist with positive attitude when enduring prolonged adversity. Living these qualities has a notable effect on those in our lives. Healing and spiritually based self-help groups operate at this level of consciousness as do saints, spiritual healers, and advanced spiritual students.

At the energy level in the high 500's of energy points, we experience the world as being God's perfect creation with endless beauty. Our life progresses with little effort in accordance with Divine timing. Our will has merged with that of the Divine and we are living from faith being led by the Divine. We see the Divine's influence more so in our life. We are aware that we are being carried along in the hands of the Divine as we live in heavenly ways. Our view and expectation of reality has shifted, and we are able to see signs in our life from the Divine that we are on the right path.

We are aware that we are but a vessel for Divine influx (Love and Wisdom) and that we do nothing of our own. Our outlook on life has shifted further in that we have an even greater ambition to use our state of being for the benefit of life itself rather than to benefit just some individuals. We now have a greater ability to love many people than before and with more power. Interestingly, some people who have suffered near-death experiences have been temporarily subjected to energy levels in the range 540 to 600 points.

Energy level 600 points is Peace, associated with experiences designated by terms such as transcendence, self-realisation, and God-consciousness. It is extremely rare for people to reach consciousness energy levels of 600 points and over. At this level of consciousness life occurs in a kind of slow motion where time and space are experienced a little differently than when we are at the lower levels. We see the world as very much alive and vibrant and experience an ever-present unfolding of life that is not being processed rationally in our mind. We are now perceiving life much more intuitively. The background chatter in our mind has stopped and we are experiencing a lovely peaceful stillness in our mind as an accompaniment to our activities. We have an absolute understanding or faith that it is the infinite power of the Divine that is creating all life and giving us our perception (intuition). We realise that the loving Life from the Divine flows into all life and therefore we are connected to everything else by way of the Divine's Love and Wisdom. Only one in many million people reaches energy level 600 points and over.

Energy level 700 to 1,000 points is Enlightenment, whereby at this level we have overcome our ego or proprium (which provides us with a false sense of being separate from all of creation) and we now see our connection with God, others, and all life. We don't see our physical body as being us. Our body is seen to be a vehicle for our spirit to make use of in the physical world. Our awareness is not localised as before and is now more widely felt. We identify our self as being a conduit for the Divine to work through our being. We experience complete oneness with the Divine and a level of peace that is ineffable - beyond words.

People who have reached this level of consciousness have originated spiritual patterns and generated attractor energy fields that have influenced vast numbers of people throughout history. This level of consciousness calibrates up to 1,000 energy points, the highest level attained by any people recorded throughout history. These people are the Great Ones or Avatars with the title "Lord," who are all associated with Divinity. They include Lord Krishna, Lord Buddha, and Lord Jesus Christ.

6.3 The modern progression of consciousness

In his book *Power vs. Force*, Dr. Hawkins explains that most people don't change their level of consciousness by much over their lifetime. Their cumulative life choices can often result in a net lowering of their level of consciousness. The level of consciousness of the overall population is dragged down by vast numbers of people at lower levels. However, the overall level of consciousness of the whole population is boosted by the influence of the minority having high levels of consciousness. This is because the logarithmic scale of the energy levels of consciousness means that the positive power a person has at higher levels of consciousness is vastly times greater than a person at the lower levels. The statistical average advance for the population at large is about five energy points over a lifetime. The implication of this is that for human civilisation, consciousness evolves very slowly from generation to generation.

Dr. Hawkins explains that higher levels can be attained if we can truly overcome the dominance of our ego. We need to use our will to generally overcome our selfishness by choosing a friendly, earnest, kind, compassionate, and forgiving approach to life. As explained earlier, it is even possible for us to make sudden increases of over a hundred energy points by overcoming extremely strong temptations. We do this by living our faith to consistently reject our selfish desires. In Swedenborg's terms we make love to God and love to others our main focus as we consistently grow spiritually to become a more loving and wise person. As we do this, we express more of our true self through our personality, and we express greater heavenly power in our life. Ultimately, our life is in closer alignment with our true life purpose. We benefit more so as do those people and all creation associated with us in our life.

7 The Spiritual Dimension

The spiritual and physical worlds have been created by a supreme infinite being we call the Divine or God. Creation occurs as a result of God's Love and Wisdom in Divine order and in accordance with Divine laws and principles. Creation takes place in the spiritual universe or spiritual world with its effects being made manifest in the physical universe or physical world. Ultimately, God has created these worlds so that human beings and spirits can exist for Him to love and to bless them with peace, joy, and intense happiness. The spiritual world comprises heaven, hell, and the world of spirits where our spirits reside while we are alive in the physical world. The spiritual and physical worlds, and all life and objects within them, are kept in existence by a continual flow of life from God into creation.

7.1 The spiritual world

Swedenborg explains in his book *Heaven and Hell*, that the spiritual world is not removed and far away from this world, but rather is another dimension of consciousness. So, it is here now, and it feels more real to its inhabitants than the physical world did. Heaven and hell are not places 'here or there'. They are *states* of life. One is a state of love towards others, God, and all creation; the other is a state of selfishness.

The outward appearance of the spiritual world reflects the states of its inhabitants, being angels and evil spirits (and our spirits while we are alive in the physical world). Angels experience beautiful surrounds which are a representation of their collective inner states. Evil spirits experience barren, desolate, troubled environments, also a representation of their collective inner states. In the spiritual world, time and space are experienced differently to the physical world we live in. Angels and evil spirits are present with whomever they love to be with in an instant, and for this reason they do not experience time and space in the same way as we do in the physical world.

Our spirit is continually in company with spirits in the spiritual world; these spirits are angels and evil spirits that are connected and associated with us and also those spirits of people living with us whom we have a relationship with. Spirits communicate using a universal language that directly represents their innermost affections or desires and thoughts. They cannot communicate one thing and think and feel another. Since our spirit is in association with spirits in the spiritual world, we are also with them in spiritual thought and speech, because our mind is inwardly spiritual and outwardly in the physical world. Our soul receives influx directly from God. However, our mind is a vessel that constantly receives influx directly from God via our soul and indirectly from heaven and hell via angels and evil spirits associated with us. This allows us to feel and think and have our physical body function. Swedenborg states that if all connection and association with angels and evil spirits was taken away from us, we would die instantly since our mind would no longer function.

Angels receive influx from God that passes down from the celestial heaven to the spiritual heaven, and then to the spiritual-natural heaven, and then to the hells into every individual therein. In our physical life we receive influx from both the heavens and the hells in order that we have freewill and can develop spiritually. Our intention determines whether heavenly or hellish influx enters our lower mind and is acted on. But the life which flows into an angel or evil spirit is received differently; angels receive goodness and truth as goodness and truth; evil spirits receive goodness and truth which they turn into evil and falsity.

There is continuous interaction between our world and angels and evil spirits in the spiritual world. Some people at very critical stages in their lives have felt, seen, or heard angels with them. This is particularly so in times of extreme distress and at death. Other times some of us have felt a 'cold' presence around us being evil spirits, or even seen ghosts and 'appearances' of other kinds. Then there are those people who have undergone a 'near death experience' where their spirit leaves their physical body. Some have witnessed events remotely that went on during this time and have gone on to accurately recount these experiences upon consciously returning to their physical body.

People are mostly unaware of the continuing interaction between the two worlds, but it is nevertheless very real. The thin veil between the physical and spiritual worlds allows many instances of spirits that influence or come into contact with this world. We sometimes hear people speak of a spirit lingering around their home or workplace. This is simply because the spirit is very attached to the physical world. Eventually, either sooner or later, these lingering spirits move to a community in heaven or hell. Angels guard us when we are asleep or protect us even when we are not aware. Many people experience the sense of a guardian angel or conversely evil forces at play in their life. This is all symptomatic of these phenomena.

Swedenborg explains that in the spiritual world, those of similar affections or desires are drawn together, for that is the power of love. The selfish are not condemned to go to hell; they are drawn there by their own desires to be with others that share the same ruling love. In their eyes, in their experience, it is their own little heaven. They could not feel at ease anywhere else. We can't belong to any other 'club' than the one which reflects our character, our love. The answer lies "within you" as Jesus said so clearly, and the outer space will only be a reflection of our inner state.

It is very difficult for us as finite human beings to fully comprehend what eternal life is like. The nice thing about life in heaven is that angels constantly feel satisfied and useful without the restrictions of a frail physical body. After death we can live in a state of peace, joy, and intense happiness. Conversely, we can live in a selfish and shallow hellish world continuously wishing to have dominion over and take from others while at the same time being dominated, manipulated, or tormented by our fellow inhabitants.

7.2 Heaven

Swedenborg explains that Heaven comprises heavenly states of being rather than places that are 'above' us. Heaven is made from the divine nature of Love and Wisdom, or on a finer scale, Goodness and Truth emanating from God flowing into angels and accepted by them. The influx from God flows indirectly to angels, starting from the highest angelic heavenly communities and flowing down to the lower angelic communities. Angels are in a heavenly state to the extent that they accept this influx. Love and Wisdom from God unites angels to God and to each other. Love and

Wisdom is the essential reality and the source of life of angels.

The whole of heaven is comprised of countless communities in three heavens: the celestial heaven, spiritual heaven, and the spiritual-natural heaven. The angels in the celestial heaven are closest to God and love Him more than anything in that they love His Goodness more than anything. They perceive truth intuitively and are the most loving, wise, and innocent. Angels in the spiritual heaven rationalise truth and love God's Wisdom more than anything. Angels in the spiritual-natural heaven follow rules and love to lead good moral lives more than anything. The celestial heaven is the most perfect followed by the spiritual heaven and lastly the spiritual-natural heaven.

> **Love in the heavens:**
>
> Swedenborg, *Heaven and Hell*
>
> In the heavens there is a sharing of all with each and of each with all. Such sharing goes forth from the two loves of heaven, which are: love to God and love towards others, and to share their delight is the very nature of these loves.

The landscape of heaven is a reflection of the overall communal effect of its inhabitant's inner states of peace, contentment, love to others and life, and love to God. The one corresponds to the other. It is from this that heaven has its beauty and tranquillity. As well, it is in heaven that all can have the intense happiness with which God wishes to bless our lives. Angels live in loving communities with homes, gardens, countryside, and places of work, similar to our physical world except that all aspects of their environment are much more beautiful, ordered, and peaceful, changing as an outer reflection of individual and collective inner states. Just as their environment is a reflection of their states, so too are their clothes.

Whilst certainly heaven is a place of peace and joy, it is not 'a doing nothing' place. Heaven is a kingdom of uses. Would you like to do nothing forever? As such, angels are involved in numerous activities and tasks they love to do, all related to ensuring the greatest perfection and happiness for the whole of heaven and our world – no unemployment there! Everyone there is supremely happy, employed in a way for which he or she is uniquely fit and ideally suited to. Work is not regarded as drudgery as is so often the case here. It is a delight to be of use and service in whatever role they play. Special functions include caring for young children who have died and educating newly arrived persons from this world. In heaven the sick and the physically and intellectually disabled are restored to full health. The aged grow younger and those who died as babies and children are cared for with great love by angels and so grow to maturity as angels.

Heaven:

Swedenborg, *Heaven and Hell*

One can see how great the delight of heaven must be from the fact that it is the delight of everyone in heaven to share their delights and blessings with others.

All are born for heaven. The people who passed on and ended up in heaven are those when in the physical world mostly chose goodness throughout their life, and as such

128

have developed a heavenly ruling love. In heaven they wish and continue to be of greatest use to all, performing uses that they innately love.

7.3 Hell

Swedenborg explains that hell comprises states of being rather than places that are 'below' us. There are three hells that are opposites to the three heavens; the deepest hell is where the worst evil spirits known as genii reside; the middle hell is where evil spirits known as devils reside; and the highest hell is where the least-worst evil spirits known as satans reside.

The hells vary in appearance from dark forests where hellish spirits roam like wild beasts, to barren sandy deserts with rugged cliffs and dark caves, to swamps and stagnant ponds. Areas in the milder hells have crude huts or ruined houses that look burnt-out and are scattered about and grouped into what resembles cities with alleyways and streets. The hellish spirits in these homes subject each other to constant quarrelling, hostility, beating, theft, and violence.

Divine Truth has total and absolute power in the spiritual world. As such, the hells are governed by a flow of Divine Good and Divine Truth from God via the heavens that restrains and controls the general effort flowing out of the hells. Sometimes angels are sent there so that their presence will act to restrain and control its inhabitant's propensity for evil. In addition, the more malevolent evil spirits use their experience and skill to keep the rest of their community in servile obedience by punishments and the fears that these punishments give rise to. These dominant spirits do not dare go beyond fixed limits.

After our death, and according to what our spirit becomes as a result of our moment-to-moment choices during our physical life, we will automatically seek out others like ourselves, either in heaven or in hell. God does not judge spirits and send them to hell as punishment. If our dominant love is selfish, we will seek out a community of evil spirits that share our ruling love. Evil spirits bring punishment and suffering upon themselves and others in their community through their evil desires, thoughts, and actions. And yet they endure this because they love those evils so much and derive great pleasure and satisfaction from exercising them.

Hell is not the place of physical torment that many people think it to be. It is where spirits, who reject the love of God and who lived mostly a selfish physical life, choose to be. To them this is 'heaven' or paradise. All will live to eternity, and it is God's will that we shall do so in heaven. He, in His mercy, allows hell to exist for those who, because of their own selfishness, would find the unselfish love of life in heaven intolerable. But He doesn't shut them out of heaven. They simply loathe being there and instead gravitate towards others that have the same selfish ruling love. Heaven is always open to those who have a heavenly ruling love and will therefore be happy there. At various times God is asked by some evil spirits what heaven is like. He sometimes grants their wishes by briefly placing them in heaven to show them its beauty. Heaven does not fit for them, and while there they feel intense pain and discomfort, and so promptly return to their hellish community.

7.4 Angels and evil spirits

Angels are as human in form and appearance in the spiritual world as they were in the physical world but more beautiful.

However, the true form of evil spirits is monstrous, each spirit being in a form depending on their degree and type of evil nature. This is how angels see them. By God's grace, evil spirits appear to each other as humans and not as monsters.

Angels and evil spirits have all their faculties, senses, characteristics, and memory. Every angel and evil spirit has a body with head, eyes, ears, torso, arms, hands, and feet – of spiritual substances more real and responsive than physical substances. They communicate using a universal language which conveys their innermost thoughts and affections (in the case of angels) or hatreds (in the case of evil spirits).

7.4.1 Angels

The term *Angel* is derived from the Greek word Angelos, meaning "a messenger" or "one who is sent". Swedenborg very clearly informs us that angels are not a separate creation of God. They are beings that have lived a human life and development as we do. They tended to consciously strive in the physical world to live their lives in service to God and to others for the greatest good for all. As such, we are all potential angels.

> **Guardian angels:**
>
> Swedenborg, *Divine Love and Wisdom*
>
> At least two guardian angels are constantly with us, a celestial angel and a spiritual angel (and at least two evil spirits). It is this presence bringing teaching, healing and comfort, of which we can become directly aware. Although, when we are in a selfish state of mind, we draw evil spirits close to us and the angels with us back away.

Angels are influencing our inner life, seeking to develop, strengthen, and protect us and others. They gently influence us and bend us towards good. Conversely, evil spirits influence our inner life inducing fear in an attempt to weaken, confuse, and destroy us and others. Note that both angels and evil spirits seek to bring people into the same love and life that they have and enjoy. Angels experience vastly greater levels of goodness, wisdom, and innocence than we do in the physical world. Wisdom is their spiritual nourishment, and they are continually being perfected in wisdom to eternity. They wear clothes that are a perfect representation of their wisdom and intelligence, and as their inner states change, so do their clothes. They ultimately live as committed couples either with the partner they truly loved in this world or with one having a deeply complementary nature.

A special role of angels is their ministry with each individual in this world protecting us (so far as we allow them) against selfish desires and thoughts coming from the activity of evil spirits. They do this by bringing counterbalancing influences leading us to make spiritually healthy choices. We are generally unconscious of this process except when our conscience is troubled by difficult spiritual choices. When we do make spiritually healthy choices, the love and wisdom from angels flows into our minds and we experience loving emotions, feelings, thoughts, and actions.

7.4.2 Evil spirits

Swedenborg explains that as with angels, evil spirits have been people in the physical world; however, they have mostly chosen evil over good. They were people in this world who gained satisfaction and pleasure when controlling and influencing others for their own benefit and wanted to be worshipped or idolised. They were also people whose love in life was to be served by others, to selfishly pursue material possessions, and to cause mischief. These traits are continued in the spiritual world where these spirits take great delight in trying to control and destructively influence their fellow inhabitants and people in this world. This is the reason they are called evil spirits, because they desire evil.

Evil spirits receive goodness and truth from God via the heavens but either reject, suffocate, or pervert it so that it becomes evil and falsity. They enter all things in our memory to cause mischief and harm to us. They only attack those things that relate to our heavenly life (eternal life), being our heavenly love and wisdom, goodness and truth. They are drawn closer to our spirit when we choose to be selfish and will infiltrate our minds to create disorder and lead us away from God. When we go against our conscience and give in to the constant temptations from evil spirits, we restrict and distort some of the flow of goodness and truth from our higher mind. We also take their evil and falsity into our lower mind which corrupts it, and this delights them the most. In doing this, we allow evil spirits to control us as this happens. Later, should we draw upon their influence, we undergo a further cycle as they stir up this acquired evil and falsity so they can dominate and control us. This leads to the generation of negative emotions such as guilt, shame, anger, anxiety, despair, and fear and unhealthy thoughts and actions.

7.5 Death

We are essentially spiritual beings in human form during our physical life. As explained previously, we are not our body, we are our mind. Our life in the physical world allows us to be subjected to freewill so that we have the opportunity to grow spiritually. In order to live in the physical world, we need a physical body, which is the lowest order in our creation. Influx flows from God into our soul and is transformed by our higher mind; this influx is then passed into and transformed by our lower mind; then this influx is passed into and transformed by our auric field which ultimately manifests our physical body.

Eventually we reach the time in our physical life when our physical body dies, although we don't die. At our death our soul with spirit disconnects from our 'invisible physical body' and physical body. Our 'invisible physical body' is formed from the first three bodies of our auric field (etheric body, emotional body, and mental body) and the lower three chakras. Then these three auric bodies and lower three chakras dissipate and dissolve, and our physical body decomposes. What remains is our soul and spirit (comprising our higher mind, lower mind, and our spiritual body). Our spiritual body comprises bodies four to seven of our auric field (relational body, higher intent body, higher love body, and higher mind body) with their nadis/meridians and chakras. We also maintain cord connections with those people in the physical world and spirits with whom we have had a relationship. Now we gently become conscious of the spiritual world where we go on living and developing as a spirit – although our ruling love does not change.

Swedenborg explains that when we have passed into the spiritual world, we will have all our faculties, senses, characteristics and memory. What we call death is our transition from one world to the other. And it is as much within the Divine order and scheme of things as birth is. By birth we come into this world, whereas at death we gently come into conscious awareness of the spiritual world.

> **The three stages we pass through after death:**
>
> Swedenborg, *Heaven and Hell*
>
> *Stage 1:* Awareness of the spiritual world and our physical life at a relatively external level.
>
> *Stage 2:* Exposure to our inward (true) self and our ruling love being either heavenly or hellish in nature.
>
> *Stage 3:* Instruction for heaven for those who have a heavenly ruling love.

Everyone after passing into the spiritual world is given a review of their life and choices. Even for the case of an atheist who professes no belief in God, there is an opportunity to affirm a belief in God from insights received as their life in the spiritual world unfolds. Many atheists lead full, useful, moral and productive lives, and can ultimately acknowledge God. During this process, a spirit's thinking becomes less and less materialistic. In general, the experience of life in the spiritual world is similar to life here, except that the environment of the spiritual world becomes a true reflection of the delights and affections or hatreds of the spirits who are there.

Eventually after passing on, a spirit's true self and delight (ruling love) developed during their physical life gradually emerges and is clearly revealed. The spirit will have developed their nature or ruling love as a result of the choices they made throughout their life in the physical world. When this process is complete, the spirit will naturally gravitate towards others of similar delights and enter either the life of heaven or the life of hell. God does not judge spirits and send them to hell as punishment.

Further explanation of the stages we pass through after death:

Stage 1: Initially, after we die, we barely recognise that we are no longer in the physical world. One aspect that strikes us as different is the fact that we are experiencing a period of rejoicing and reunion as we meet friends and relatives who have passed over before us. During this time our spirit is in a relatively external state as we reflect on our life in the physical world. This reflection includes being made aware of our thinking about external things, our conscience, and our life at a relatively external level. This allows us to assess the way we lived at a superficial level and how we have dealt with our life. During this period, we are experiencing and adjusting to our spiritual body. We are also becoming familiar with some aspects of the spiritual world.

Stage 2: The second stage goes to a much deeper or interior level. We are progressively exposed to what we really were inwardly, what type of choices we made during our life - whether loving or evil. In other words, what our ruling love is, not what we showed outwardly but what we thought inwardly. In the physical world this can be contradictory, but in preparation for heaven or hell we must face up to who and what we truly are. This goes to the heart of our being or our spirit and whether we truly wanted to be loving and wise or were deliberately evil and mostly interested in self. This state is progressively opened to us. Some spirits are so angelic that they pass almost immediately to heaven after death, and some so evil that they go almost immediately to hell. However, the majority spend varying times in this intermediate stage 'finding their true selves'.

Stage 3: The third stage involves instruction for heaven by angels and the removal of the cruder elements of a spirit's desires and thoughts and their purification. This is only given to those spirits with a heavenly ruling love who have dominant qualities of love, wisdom, and care for others, God, and all life. For those spirits who love evil rather than good, the second stage is all there is before making their home in hell because of the evils they delight in. Those spirits that are destined for heaven are instructed by angels so that they can be shown the true heavenly state and the way of life in the community to which they will go. Through God's Grace, all 'new' spirits, being angels and evil spirits, go to a community that satisfies their ruling love.

Conclusion

The seven chapters of this book have covered a broad overview of spirituality and life, and explained spiritual concepts and principles so we can apply them in our daily life. We have come to understand that God with His infinite and all-powerful qualities of Love and Wisdom, has created us and the spiritual and physical universes for us to live in. He is continuous and infinite in all ways, uncreated, always was, Eternal, unchanging, all-knowing, all-present, all-powerful, Being, and Life itself. He gives us life in this world so we have the opportunity to evolve spiritually through freewill under His Providence, so He can gift us with finite aspects of His heavenly qualities to make us truly human.

God has created each of us with a soul, higher mind, lower mind, an invisible auric field containing seven invisible bodies (from which our physical body manifests), and chakras and nadis/meridians that are integral to our energetic system. We have come to understand that our spirit comprises our mind and spiritual body, with our mind made up of several separate levels and degrees that ultimately work effectively together. We as human beings have gifts and talents given to us by God to make good use of in our lives to best serve our 'community'.

We learnt about the spiritual laws of Providence and Freewill which respectively govern our existence for the greatest good of all and allow us to evolve spiritually. We have come to know that it is God's wish that we act with courage and choose His heavenly influx when making choices in our life. This allows God to gift us with use of His heavenly qualities of love and wisdom, goodness and truth in our mind. These Divine gifts at all times belong to God.

We have come to understand that God's Life or Consciousness, being His Love and Wisdom, perpetually emanates throughout the spiritual and physical universes. Love provides the motivating energy and substance to create, while wisdom is the means to manifest, with good use being the end goal and result that is loved. Love is comprised of related and ordered affections or goodness as is wisdom comprised of related and ordered truths, with goodness motivating truth. We need to learn truth by rationalising or understanding it, and grow to love acting by it to become a more loving and wise person.

We learnt that when we live our life following God, He gives us His Love and Wisdom directly into our mind and also indirectly via the angels with us. In our lower mind, love resides in our will and works with wisdom in our understanding. We feel pangs of conscience whenever we fail to resist evil desires and go against our conscience. Doing so restricts influx from our higher mind and corrupts God's love and wisdom in our lower mind. This increases evil and falsity in our lower mind. We grow spiritually when we successfully resist selfish desires over time, and when this happens God gives us more of His love and wisdom, goodness and truth into our mind, developing our heavenly proprium and conscience.

We have come to learn that the cyclic spiritual growth process involves the three stages of repentance, reformation, and regeneration. Repentance takes place when we become aware of our selfishness, with our attitude shifting so that we decide to work to overcome it. Reformation happens as we consistently resist our selfish desires during our periods of temptation. Eventually this culminates in a final temptation battle as evil spirits attack

God's goodness and truth in us while God defends these heavenly qualities in us as we battle alongside God with intent. God gives us peace and consolation after we succeed with our final battle of temptation. This is followed by regeneration when God gives us more goodness and truth along with joy, and reorders the love and wisdom, goodness and truth in our mind. Goodness and truth are received and united during repentance, reformation, and more so during regeneration. As this takes place, our higher mind is ever more opened, and its quality and potency is enhanced. This allows more influx from our higher mind to flow and be transformed with greater power into our lower mind, then into our auric field, and finally into our physical body. Our higher mind, lower mind, auric field, and physical body are all enhanced. Our whole being is transformed and vibrates at a higher frequency and with greater coherency. As a result, we receive a more heavenly proprium, conscience, nature, greater wisdom and perception, a higher proportion of positive emotions, and greater physical health.

God's infinite life energy being His Love and Wisdom or Consciousness, includes a record of all existence. Some of this life energy passes through our being as we live. Our mind allows us to perceive some of this Life as states of consciousness that are but a small aspect of overall Consciousness. Our states of consciousness are temporary whereas our level of consciousness is semi-permanent and represents our actual milestone of spiritual growth. As we evolve spiritually, our level of consciousness increases as we become ever more loving, wise, and aware of the greater reality. This means that we can see the world more truly for what it really is, good and bad, and with greater hope.

Finally, we learnt that throughout our physical life we are developing our ruling or dominant love, which at the time of our death determines which spiritual community we will live in. We also gained knowledge of the spiritual world, its inhabitants, and an appreciation of life in the heavens and the hells. If when we pass on, we have a selfish ruling love, we will live a selfish life in hell. In this case we will suffer from the evils of those around us who share the same ruling love of evil and love to exercise it against us and others as we do against them. If when we pass on, we have an angelic ruling love, we will live a joyful and peaceful life of good use, love to others and love to God in heaven doing what we love most for the greatest good of all.

It has been a labour of love for me to write this book. I hope that while reading it, you have gained a good understanding and appreciation of the fundamentals of spirituality, and how this knowledge relates to our daily existence. May you be inspired to be courageous in applying these learnings and insights throughout the remainder of your life for great benefit, blessings, and substantial spiritual growth along your journey.

Bibliography

Belòt, H., *The Language of the Body*, Belòt, 2004

Brennan, B., *Hands of Light*, Barbara A. Brennan, 1987

Brennan, B., *Light Emerging*, Bantam New Age Books, 1993

Gladish, D., *Love in Marriage*, Swedenborg Foundation, 1992

Hawkins, D., *Power vs Force*, Hay House, 2012

Kingslake, B., *Swedenborg Explores The Spiritual Dimension*, Swedenborg Association of Australia, 1984

Klein, J.T., *The Power of Service*, J. Appleseesd & Co., 1998

Krebs, C., and O'Neill McGowan, T., *Energy Kinesiology*, Handspring Publishing Limited, 2014

Lazer, B., *Temptations*, Lazer, 1996

Odhner, H.L., *The Human Mind*, Swedenborg Scientific Association Bryn Athyn, 1969

Pettinelli, M., *The Psychology of Emotions*, Feelings and Thoughts, Pettinelli, 2012

Stanley, M., *Emanuel Swedenborg Essential Readings*, The Swedenborg Lending Library and Enquiry Centre, 1993

Swedenborg, E., *Secrets of Heaven*, Swedenborg Foundation, 1998

Swedenborg, E., *Conjugial Love*, Swedenborg Foundation, 2009

Swedenborg, E., *Divine Love and Wisdom*, The Swedenborg Society, 1987

Swedenborg, E., *Divine Providence*, Swedenborg Foundation, 2009

Swedenborg, E., *Heaven and Hell*, Swedenborg Foundation, 2002

Swedenborg, E., *New Jerusalem and Its Heavenly Doctrine*, Swedenborg Foundation, 2009

http://swedenborg.com.au, *The Swedenborg Programme*, 38

Taylor, D., *The Hidden Levels of the Mind*, Swedenborg Foundation Press, 1982

Van Dusen, W., *The Presence of Other Worlds*, Chrysalis Books, 2004

Warren, S.M., *Compendium of Swedenborg's Theological Writings*, Swedenborg Society, 1939

Wilber, K., *Integral Spirituality*, Integral Books, 2007